Programming Razor

Programming Razor

Jess Chadwick

Beijing · Cambridge · Farnham · Köln · Sebastopol · Tokyo

Programming Razor

by Jess Chadwick

Copyright © 2011 Chadwick Software, LLC. All rights reserved.
Printed in the United States of America.

Published by O'Reilly Media, Inc., 1005 Gravenstein Highway North, Sebastopol, CA 95472.

O'Reilly books may be purchased for educational, business, or sales promotional use. Online editions are also available for most titles (*http://my.safaribooksonline.com*). For more information, contact our corporate/institutional sales department: (800) 998-9938 or *corporate@oreilly.com*.

Editors: Shawn Wallace and Mike Hendrickson	**Cover Designer:** Karen Montgomery
Production Editor: Teresa Elsey	**Interior Designer:** David Futato
	Illustrator: Robert Romano

Revision History for the First Edition:

2001-09-28   First release

See *http://oreilly.com/catalog/errata.csp?isbn=9781449306762* for release details.

ISBN: 978-1-449-30676-2

[LSI]

1317220070

To my father, for sparking my lifelong passion for twiddling bits and bytes.

To my wife, for putting up with my lifelong passion for bits and bytes twiddling.

Table of Contents

Preface

Razor is a scripting syntax that simplifies the way you create dynamic, data-driven websites. In this book, you'll build example websites with Microsoft WebMatrix and ASP.NET MVC and learn how Razor lets you combine code and content in a fluid and expressive manner on Windows-based servers. We'll also explore components of the Razor API and see how Razor templates are turned into rendered HTML. By the end of this book, you'll be able to create Razor-based websites with custom extensions that meet the specific needs of your projects.

RazorPad: A Lightweight Razor Editor

The Razor syntax is designed to be written and executed within development environments such as WebMatrix and Visual Studio. This book provides instructions on how to download and install both of these applications.

However, if you are not interested in or able to install additional software on your computer, the author has created an application named RazorPad, which allows you to enter, edit, and execute Razor snippets outside of bulky development environments.

RazorPad is available in two flavors:

Online, browser-based editor
> RazorPad is hosted online at *http://razorpad.net*. The online editor provides a sandbox for you to test out your Razor snippets and see the resulting rendered output right in your browser.

Stand-alone application
> For those who prefer "rich clients," RazorPad is also available as a small stand-alone WPF application that does not require any installation. You can download the RazorPad WPF application from *http://razorpad.codeplex.com*.

Conventions Used in This Book

The following typographical conventions are used in this book:

Italic

 Indicates new terms, URLs, email addresses, filenames, and file extensions.

`Constant width`

 Used for program listings, as well as within paragraphs to refer to program elements such as variable or function names, databases, data types, environment variables, statements, and keywords.

`Constant width bold`

 Shows commands or other text that should be typed literally by the user.

`Constant width italic`

 Shows text that should be replaced with user-supplied values or by values determined by context.

 This icon signifies a tip, suggestion, or general note.

 This icon indicates a warning or caution.

Using Code Examples

This book is here to help you get your job done. In general, you may use the code in this book in your programs and documentation. You do not need to contact us for permission unless you're reproducing a significant portion of the code. For example, writing a program that uses several chunks of code from this book does not require permission. Selling or distributing a CD-ROM of examples from O'Reilly books does require permission. Answering a question by citing this book and quoting example code does not require permission. Incorporating a significant amount of example code from this book into your product's documentation does require permission.

We appreciate, but do not require, attribution. An attribution usually includes the title, author, publisher, and ISBN. For example: "*Programming Razor* by Jess Chadwick (O'Reilly). Copyright 2011 Chadwick Software, LLC, 978-1-449-30676-2."

If you feel your use of code examples falls outside fair use or the permission given above, feel free to contact us at *permissions@oreilly.com*.

Safari® Books Online

 Safari Books Online is an on-demand digital library that lets you easily search over 7,500 technology and creative reference books and videos to find the answers you need quickly.

With a subscription, you can read any page and watch any video from our library online. Read books on your cell phone and mobile devices. Access new titles before they are available for print, and get exclusive access to manuscripts in development and post feedback for the authors. Copy and paste code samples, organize your favorites, download chapters, bookmark key sections, create notes, print out pages, and benefit from tons of other time-saving features.

O'Reilly Media has uploaded this book to the Safari Books Online service. To have full digital access to this book and others on similar topics from O'Reilly and other publishers, sign up for free at *http://my.safaribooksonline.com*.

How to Contact Us

Please address comments and questions concerning this book to the publisher:

O'Reilly Media, Inc.
1005 Gravenstein Highway North
Sebastopol, CA 95472
800-998-9938 (in the United States or Canada)
707-829-0515 (international or local)
707-829-0104 (fax)

We have a web page for this book, where we list errata, examples, and any additional information. You can access this page at:

http://www.oreilly.com/catalog/0636920020622/

To comment or ask technical questions about this book, send email to:

bookquestions@oreilly.com

For more information about our books, courses, conferences, and news, see our website at *http://www.oreilly.com*.

Find us on Facebook: *http://facebook.com/oreilly*

Follow us on Twitter: *http://twitter.com/oreillymedia*

Watch us on YouTube: *http://www.youtube.com/oreillymedia*

CHAPTER 1

Introduction

HyperText Markup Language (HTML) makes the World Wide Web possible. Every website uses HTML to render content, and much of HTML's popularity derives from its simplicity: with knowledge of just a few concepts, anyone can publish content to the Web.

HTML may be a way of life for web developers, but when it comes to creating dynamic, data-driven websites, most developers turn to some kind of tool to make the job of generating HTML easier. Razor is one of those tools: a scripting syntax for making templates and web content on Windows-based web servers.

This book is designed to get you acquainted with the Razor syntax and how it fits into the two primary Microsoft development environments: ASP.NET MVC and WebMatrix. The final chapters will dive deeper, cracking open the underlying tooling and API to see what makes this all possible. By the end of this book, not only will you know how to create great Razor-based websites, but you will also be able to add custom extensions and make Razor even better suited to the specific needs of your projects!

A Brief History of Microsoft's Web Development Platforms

Long ago, Microsoft saw the need for a Windows-based web development platform and worked hard to produce a solution. Over the last two decades, Microsoft has given the development community several web development platforms.

Active Server Pages (ASP)

Microsoft's first answer to web development was Active Server Pages (ASP), a scripting language in which code and markup are authored together in a single file, with each physical file corresponding to a page on the website. ASP's server-side scripting approach became widely popular and many websites grew out of it; some continue to serve visitors today! After a while, though, developers wanted more: things like easier code reuse, better separation of concerns, and easier application of object-oriented programming principles. In 2002, Microsoft offered ASP.NET as a solution to these concerns.

ASP.NET Web Forms

Like ASP websites, ASP.NET websites rely on the page-based approach, where each page on the website is represented in the form of a physical file (called a Web Form) and is accessible using that file's name. Unlike a page using ASP, a Web Forms page provides some separation of code and markup by splitting the web content into two different files: one for the code and one for the markup. ASP.NET and the Web Forms approach served developers' needs for years and continues to be the web development framework of choice for many .NET developers. Some .NET developers, however, consider the Web Forms approach too much of an abstraction from the underlying HTML, JavaScript, and CSS. Gee, some developers just can't be pleased! Or can they?

ASP.NET MVC

Microsoft was quick to spot the growing need in the ASP.NET developer community for something different from the page-based Web Forms approach, and it released the first version of ASP.NET MVC in 2008. Representing a total departure from the Web Forms approach, ASP.NET MVC abandons the page-based architecture completely, using a Model-View-Controller (MVC) architecture instead. Though it still leverages much of the previous framework, ASP.NET MVC represents an entirely separate stack. Instead of markup files, *views* take the responsibility for rendering HTML to the user. ASP.NET MVC leaves it up to application developers to choose the syntax they use to author views. Razor is quickly emerging as the most popular ASP.NET MVC view syntax for reasons that should become quite clear while reading this book!

WebMatrix

Released at the same time as ASP.NET MVC 3 in early 2011, WebMatrix is Microsoft's simple, straightforward, and free web development environment. Comprising a simple integrated development environment (IDE) and an API (named Web Pages), WebMatrix is a natural fit in the evolution of Microsoft's web development frameworks. Web-Matrix offers a middle ground for those who view ASP as a hindrance to object-oriented development, ASP.NET Web Forms as too much of an abstraction from core HTML/CSS/JavaScript, and ASP.NET MVC as too complex.

At a glance, WebMatrix web pages bear a strong resemblance to ASP web pages, in that they combine business logic and markup in the same file. However, if you dig deeper, you'll quickly find a very object-oriented foundation lurking underneath. By combining the power of the ASP.NET platform with the simplicity of ASP-like scripting syntax (the Razor syntax), WebMatrix offers a web development environment that is approachable by a very broad range of website developers. WebMatrix is straightforward enough to allow a hobbyist to produce a simple website, yet powerful enough to satisfy the needs of more advanced web applications.

Hello, Razor!

Razor is a template syntax that allows you to combine code and content in a fluid and expressive manner. Though it introduces a few symbols and keywords, Razor is not a new language. Instead, Razor lets you write code using languages you probably already know, such as C# or Visual Basic .NET.

Razor's learning curve is very short, as it lets you work with your existing skills rather than requiring you to learn an entirely new language. Therefore, if you know how to write HTML and make a .NET API call, you can easily write markup like the following:

```
<div>This page rendered at @DateTime.Now</div>
```

which produces output like this:

```
<div>This page rendered at 12/7/1941 7:38:00 AM</div>
```

This example begins with a standard HTML tag (the `<div>` tag), followed by a bit of static text. In the midst of all of this is some dynamic text rendered via a call to the .NET `System.DateTime` object, followed by the closing (`</div>`) tag.

Razor's intelligent parser allows developers to be more expressive with their logic and make easier transitions between code and markup. The more advanced the markup, the easier it is to see how Razor's syntax is cleaner and more expressive than the Web Forms syntax. Compare the following scenarios, each one showing the Razor markup and Web Forms markup required to produce the same HTML:

`if/else` *statement using Web Forms syntax*

```
<% if(User.IsAuthenticated) { %>
        <span>Hello, <%= User.Username %>!</span>
<% } %>
<% else { %>
        <span>Please <%= Html.ActionLink("log in") %></span>
<% } %>
```

`if/else` *statement using Razor syntax*

```
@if(User.IsAuthenticated) {
    <span>Hello, @User.Username!</span>
} else {
    <span>Please @Html.ActionLink("log in")</span>
}
```

`foreach` *loop using Web Forms syntax*

```
<ul>
<% foreach( var post in blogPosts) { %>
    <li><a href="<%= post.Href %>"><%= post.Title %></a></li>
```

```
<% } %>
</ul>
```

foreach *loop using Razor syntax*

```
<ul>
@foreach( var post in blogPosts) {
    <li><a href="@post.Href">@post.Title</a></li>
}
</ul>
```

Though the difference between the Web Forms syntax and Razor syntax is only a few characters, those characters make a big difference in the readability of the markup! One of the loudest complaints from developers attempting to use Web Forms to author dynamic markup is that its "angle-bracket" syntax is so verbose that it can distract from the page's logic and content. Additionally, because the Web Forms syntax itself so closely resembles HTML markup, it is often difficult to determine at a glance which parts of the template are code and which are markup.

In direct contrast, Razor uses minimal markup to perform the same tasks. What's more, Razor's syntax was deliberately designed to blend in with HTML, not conflict with it.

Differentiating Code and Markup

Razor provides two ways to differentiate code from markup: *code nuggets* and *code blocks*.

Code Nuggets

Code nuggets are simple expressions that are evaluated and rendered inline. They can be mixed with text and look like this:

```
Not Logged In: @Html.ActionLink("Login", "Login")
```

The expression begins immediately after the @ symbol, and Razor is smart enough to know that the closing parenthesis indicates the end of this particular statement. The previous example will render this output:

```
Not Logged In: <a href="/Login">Login</a>
```

Notice that code nuggets must always return markup for the view to render. If you write a code nugget that does not return anything (i.e. returns void), you will receive an error when the view executes.

Code Blocks

A code block is a section of the view that contains strictly code rather than a combination of markup and code. Razor defines a code block as any section of a Razor template wrapped in @{ } characters. The @{ characters mark the beginning of the block, followed by any number of lines of code. The } character closes the code block.

Keep in mind that the code within a code block is not like code in a code nugget. It is fully-formed code that must follow the rules of the current language; for example, each line of code written in C# must include a semicolon (;) at the end, just as if it lived within a class in a .cs file.

Here is an example of a typical code block:

```
@{
    LayoutPage = "~/Views/Shared/_Layout.cshtml";
    View.Title = "Product Details for " + Model.ProductName;
}
```

Code blocks do not render anything to the page. Instead, they allow you to write arbitrary code that requires no return value. Variables defined within code blocks may be used by code nuggets in the same scope. That is, variables defined within the scope of a foreach loop or similar container will only be accessible within that container. Variables that are defined at the page level (not in any kind of container) will be accessible to any other code blocks or code nuggets in the page.

To clarify this, take a look at a view with a few variables defined at different scopes:

```
@{
    // The customer and order variables are
    // available to the entire page
    var customer = Model.Customer;
    var order = Model.Order;
}

<h1>@customer.Name' Order Details<h1>
<div class="items">
<!-- Loop through the Items property on the order variable -->
@foreach(var item in order.Items) {
    <!-- The item variable is only available within the foreach loop -->
    <div>
        <!-- A hyperlink builds a URL to the Order Item
             page using the Order ID and the Item ID -->
        <a href="/orders/@order.ID/@item.ID">@item.Name</a>
    </div>
}

<!-- This will throw an error: the item variable does not exist at this scope! -->
<div>Last Item: @item.Name</div>
</div>
```

Code blocks are a means to execute code within a template and do not render anything to the view. In direct contrast to the way that code nuggets *must* provide a return value for the view to render, the view will completely ignore values that a code block returns.

How Razor Parses Markup and Code

The @ symbol is the heart of the Razor syntax, the character that Razor uses to differentiate code from markup. The @ symbol marks a point at which the developer intends to switch from markup to code. In simple cases, no additional characters are needed to indicate when the code stops and the markup resumes. Razor's intelligent parser determines which parts of the template are code and which are markup.

What makes a valid code statement? Razor uses the following algorithm to find the end of a code statement once it reads the @ symbol trigger:

1. Read to the end of a valid identifier (i.e., a C# or VB keyword) or variable name.
2. If the next character is an opening bracket ((or [ )...
   a. Keep parsing until the corresponding closing bracket is located. Nested brackets are also tracked to avoid premature closing of a block.
   b. Loop back to #2.
3. If the next character is a . (period) *and precedes a valid identifier*, jump to #1.
4. Complete the code statement and continue processing the rest of the markup.

Razor relies on the current language's syntax to determine the end of a code statement. Razor also attempts to "read forward," checking if the upcoming content resembles code or markup. The specifics depend on the language currently in use (C# or VB).

Here's a typical Razor snippet:

```
@foreach(var item in order.Items) {
    <li>@item.Name</li>
}
```

The first line initializes the loop variables and opens the loop with an opening bracket; the second line renders markup; and the third line contains the closing bracket to end the loop. There is a clear transition between code and markup because the second line begins with an <li> tag that is clearly an HTML element and the third line is clearly the foreach loop's closing tag.

In this example there is another line of code following the initial opening foreach line:

```
@foreach(var item in order.Items) {
    var itemName = item.Name;
    <li>@itemName</li>
}
```

Since the second line follows the variable initialization C# syntax, Razor continues to correctly interpret this second line as C# code, as opposed to markup, and executes it as such. As it continues parsing, Razor correctly assumes that the third line is markup and renders it correctly. The final line is code again: the closing bracket for the foreach loop.

Disambiguating Code and Markup

Consider a third example, this time with C# generics syntax thrown into the mix:

```
@foreach(var item in order.Items) {
    var itemName = GetOrderItemName<string>(item);
    <li>@itemName</li>
}
```

In this example, the second line contains a generic parameter. While this is perfectly valid C# code, the bracket-based C# generic syntax is practically indistinguishable from HTML. Thus, the Razor parser gets confused and cannot determine whether to interpret the line as code or markup. Razor responds by giving up and throwing an exception.

While Razor's ability to differentiate between code and markup is generally impressive, this example shows that there are certainly scenarios that it cannot accurately parse. In these scenarios, there are several ways to explicitly state your intent and disambiguate code from markup.

Explicit code nuggets

The *explicit code nugget* syntax (@( )) allows you to wrap a code statement, unambiguously marking the beginning and end of the statement. The explicit code nugget syntax lets you give Razor some guidance about how your markup should be interpreted.

Here is an example in which Razor incorrectly assumes that the . in the filename extension is part of the code statement, resulting in a call to the (nonexistent) property Product.Name.jpg:

```
<img src="/products/@Product.Name.jpg" />
```

The explicit code nugget syntax clears things right up, wrapping the code to separate it from content:

```
<img src="/products/@(Product.Name).jpg" />
```

The same syntax can be applied to differentiate the generic parameter in the example at the beginning of this section. In this example, however, the preceding @ character is not required because the trouble spot is already within a code statement:

```
@foreach(var item in order.Items) {
    var itemName = ( GetOrderItemName<string>(item) );
    <li>@itemName</li>
}
```

The @: character sequence

The @: character sequence indicates a transition, telling Razor to assume that the content that follows the sequence is content, not code. You are still free to use the @ symbol any time after transitioning to content mode to execute code, just as in any other part of the Razor template. The following example shows the @: character sequence in action:

```
@if(User.IsAuthenticated) {
    @:Hello, @User.Name!
}
else {
    @:Please login
}
```

The conditional markup in this example does not specify any HTML, so it is difficult for Razor to figure out when or if to transition to markup mode. After all, how can Razor know whether "Hello" is a class name or an arbitrary word? The markup in the if condition uses the @: character sequence to specify that "Hello" is actually content and not code. The same markup then switches back to code mode to render the value of the User.Name property. The markup in the else condition also uses the @: character sequence to indicate that the text should be rendered verbatim.

The <text> block

The <text> block is an alternative to the @: character sequence that allows you to denote that an entire portion of a template is content. <text> is useful in scenarios where multiple lines of markup can be interpreted as code or text, such as:

```
@if(!User.IsAuthenticated) {
    <text>
    Guests are not allowed to view this content.
    Please @Html.ActionLink("login", "Login") to view.
    </text>
}
```

which produces the following output when the user is not authenticated:

```
Guests are not allowed to view this content.
Please <a href="/Login">login</a> to view.
```

As you can see, the opening and closing <text> tags are only used within the template to mark the beginning and end of the block of content and are not rendered along with the content. The example also shows that code statements are still perfectly acceptable within a <text> block.

There are plenty of circumstances that confuse Razor. By default, it will assume that ambiguous markup is code. Consider the @: character sequence and <text> blocks as a way to tell Razor "whenever you are unsure about whether something in this block is code or content, it is content!"

Comments

Many developers strive to write code in such a way that the code documents itself. Sometimes, however, it's not possible; perhaps there is a particularly complex bit of markup, or you need to leave a note for the next developer to come along (who might be you). Or you need to temporarily exclude a portion of a template without deleting it entirely.

To support these scenarios, Razor lets you comment out portions of markup with the @* *@ syntax. Any markup wrapped in a Razor comment block will remain in the template but will not have any effect on rendering.

Here is a simple Razor template with a few parts commented out:

```
First
@* Second *@
Third @* Fourth *@ Fifth
```

This template renders the output:

```
First

Third Fifth
```

The Second and Fourth words are not included in the output, and are completely ignored by Razor.

 Comment blocks open with the @* characters and close with the *@ characters, regardless of where they appear. Comment blocks can exclude only a small part of a line or span multiple lines.

CHAPTER 2

Razor and Microsoft WebMatrix

The previous chapter discussed Microsoft's various forays into web development platforms and editors and how each of them hits or misses with a given crowd. Microsoft WebMatrix targets a somewhat wide range of developers, but its real sweet spot is the content-driven website comprising a suite of simple yet dynamic web pages.

Introducing ASP.NET Web Pages

For easy authoring of these dynamic web pages, Microsoft introduced ASP.NET Web Pages, a straightforward page-based architecture different from existing ASP.NET technologies, such as Web Forms and ASP.NET MVC. Using the Web Pages approach, developers create their websites one page at a time, adding logic and behavior inline as needed.

This approach mimics other platforms and languages, such as PHP, but Web Pages is backed by the .NET Framework and its popular programming languages, C# and Visual Basic .NET. Using WebMatrix, developers can start with simple web pages, but when their sites require a bit more complexity, they can easily access the full power of the .NET Framework.

Installing WebMatrix

Getting started with WebMatrix is easy. First, install the application using the Web Platform Installer. To do so, navigate to the Web Platform Installer's website and look for the download link. Once in the Web Platform Installer, search through the list of available products to find the entry for WebMatrix. Click "Install," and then wait for the download and installation to finish.

Your First WebMatrix Website

One of WebMatrix's best features is that it offers myriad options for creating a new website. You may choose to start simply, with just a "normal" site (a single HTML page, some CSS, and perhaps a layout) or choose one of the many popular open source packages, such as the .NET-based Umbraco or DotNetNuke Content Management System (CMS), or even PHP-based solutions such as Joomla!, which are mere clicks away. Since you're still learning your way around, choose the basic "Empty Site" option.

After WebMatrix has created the new site, you will see a dashboard containing some information about your new site and displaying several options available to you.

The File List View

The File List view is where you will most likely spend the majority of your time in WebMatrix. This view lists the content of your site on the left side and opens up an editor on the right, allowing you to modify and customize your website. Since we selected the "Empty Site" template earlier, you'll notice that the file list is currently empty except for a single *robots.txt* file.

 The *robots.txt* file provides website developers the opportunity to describe their sites to search engines like Google and Bing. This is part of Search Engine Optimization (SEO) - a set of techniques that helps drive traffic to your site through better search rankings.

Finally, it is time to create your first web page using Razor! The easiest way to add a new page to a WebMatrix site is by using the "New" button in the toolbar, which will present you with a list of file types like those shown in Figure 2-1. Instead of selecting the normal HTML page file type (HTML) choose the CSHTML file type. CSHTML is a web page that uses the Razor syntax and the C# code language. After selecting the CSHTML option from the list of file types, specify the page name. Since this is the first page in our site, enter *Default.cshtml* in the Name field. This will create a new file of the same name in the root of your site folder, containing an HTML content template with the standard markup generated for you (see Figure 2-2). Note that at this point there is no Razor syntax in this file. It is currently pure HTML, but the fact that we chose the CSHTML file type allows us to use Razor in this page.

Website Administration

WebMatrix websites are very versatile and configurable. However, most of the configuration options are not exposed directly in the WebMatrix UI. To access the full configuration settings for a WebMatrix site, navigate to the Site section in the WebMatrix UI, and then select the ASP.NET Web Pages Administration option.

Figure 2-1. WebMatrix file types

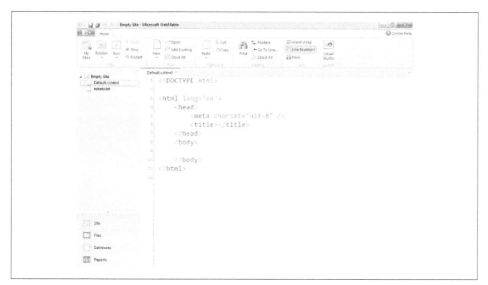

Figure 2-2. New Razor View

The ASP.NET Web Pages Administration button will open a new browser instance pointing to the administration web interface for your website. Follow the instructions provided by the interface to log in. Once you have successfully logged in, you should be able to access the full administration portal, allowing you to quickly and easily administer your site.

Hello World, Razor Style

Though Razor allows an extensive range of code to be included in a page, we will start small, with a simple code nugget indicating the current time using the .NET `Sys tem.DateTime` object. The following listing contains the required markup:

```
<!DOCTYPE html>

<html lang="en">
    <head>
        <meta charset="utf-8" />
        <title></title>
    </head>
    <body>
        The time is @DateTime.Now
    </body>
</html>
```

Now that the page has content, click the Run button in the WebMatrix toolbar to run the website for the first time. You should see the markup rendered in the browser with the `@DateTime.Now` portion replaced with the current time.

Congratulations, you have created your first Razor web page!

Data Access with WebMatrix

While the "current time" example helps show Razor in action within a WebMatrix page, real websites typically have a bit more content and logic. At its core, a weblog is just a list of content posts with metadata, which makes one a great context for beginners to use to learn the WebMatrix platform. Since WebMatrix web pages use Razor, developers have access to all of the features and functionality discussed earlier. The following sections leverage these Razor features along with WebMatrix's powerful data access technology to build a real, working blog from start to finish.

Creating a Database

The content for the blog site—the blog posts—needs to be stored somewhere. Though we could create a new static page for each individual post, this approach will quickly become difficult to maintain. Instead, our blog will rely on the out-of-the-box WebMatrix database functionality to create a local database to store the site's posts. In order to create a new database, switch to the Databases tab in your WebMatrix site, then click "Add a database to your site."

This will add a new file in the site's File List, named *Empty Site.sdf*. Rename this file to *Blog.sdf*. Directly underneath this new file, you will find an item named "Tables." Right-click on this item and select the "New table" option, which will open a new tab in your Design view, containing a grid in which you can define your database table's columns (see Figure 2-3).

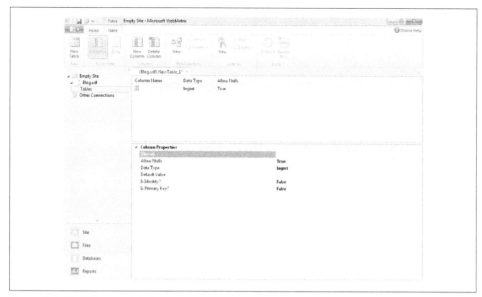

Figure 2-3. WebMatrix table designer

Use this designer to create the table that will store the blog posts. Create the columns shown in Figure 2-4.

Column Name	Data Type	Allow Nulls
ID	bigint	False
Title	nvarchar	False
PublicationDate	datetime	False
Summary	nvarchar	False
Body	ntext	False

Figure 2-4. Building the posts table

When the table definition resembles Figure 2-4, hit Ctrl-S or click the Save icon to save the new table to the database. When prompted for the table name, enter "Posts," then select "OK." That's it—you've created the blog database!

Populating the Database with Data

Before continuing on, let's add a few records to the new database so that the website has something to display when we create the rest of the site. To do this, double-click or right-click on the "Posts" table and select "Data."

The Data view, shown in Figure 2-5, allows you to view and edit the data in a database. Since this database is brand new, it does not yet have any data in it. To add data, double-click any of the editor fields (such as the field shown in Figure 2-5) and begin typing. When you are done entering data, hit Enter or click elsewhere in the application to save your changes. Add a few rows of data so that the blog pages we will soon create will have a good number of blog posts to display.

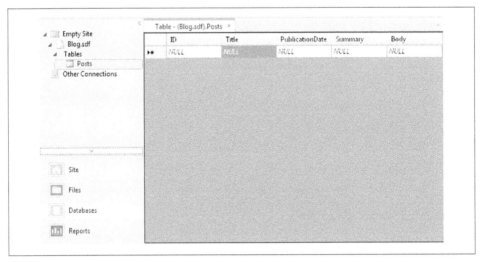

Figure 2-5. The WebMatrix database Data view

Displaying Data from the Database

Now that the database is created and has some test data in it, we can create some web pages to display that data. Before creating new files, let's take a moment to review the pages the site will need:

Add Post
> The page you'll use to add new blog posts to the database

Post
> The page that displays the full body and details of a specific blog post

Home page
> The landing page users will see when they first hit the site; it will contain a list of the most recent posts with their summaries and links to the full Post page

Creating the Add Post page

You can't have a website without some kind of content, so we may as well start out by creating the page that allows authors to post blog entries to the database for display on the site. To do this, we will create a new folder named "Posts" in the root folder of our site. (See Figure 2-6.)

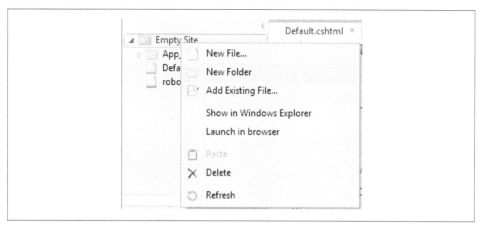

Figure 2-6. New folder context menu

Right-click on this new folder and select New File. In the New File dialog, choose the CSHTML file type and name the new file *AddPost.cshtml*.

The contents of the new file created by this wizard represent a very basic, minimal web page. This template serves as a starting point for us to add custom HTML and Razor code. We will start by adding one of the oldest and most useful tools in the HTML language: a form using the <form> tag. The <form> tag wraps a set of input fields, such as text boxes and drop-down lists, that allow users to submit data to a server for processing. The following markup will provide users with the ability to submit new blog posts:

```
<!DOCTYPE html>

<html lang="en">
    <head>
        <meta charset="utf-8" />
        <title></title>
    </head>
    <body>
      <form method="post" action="">
        <fieldset>

            <legend>New Blog Post</legend>

            <div>
                <label for="Title">Title</label>
                <input type="text" name="Title" />
            </div>

            <div>
                <label for="Summary">Summary</label>
                <input type="text" name="Summary" />
            </div>

            <div>
```

```
            <p><label for="Body">Body</label></p>
            <textarea cols="40" rows="10" name="Body">
            </textarea>
        </div>

        <div>
            <button type="submit">Add Post</button>
        </div>

    </fieldset>
  </form>
 </body>
</html>
```

What will this markup do? The opening `<form>` tag indicates to the browser what should be done with the data the user enters when he or she submits the form by clicking the submit button or hitting the Enter key. In this instance, the form will use the "POST" method (as opposed to the "GET" method) to submit the page's data back to itself.

Handling Posted Form Data

As you may have already realized, posting form data back to this page as it is now will not be very helpful; the page needs to do something with this data, such as saving it to a database. Luckily, WebMatrix provides helpers that make working with databases very easy. To reuse the page we've been working on (*AddPost.cshtml*) to save the posted form to the database, the page must be updated to extract the form data from the request, and then execute a database query to save that data.

The following snippet—placed at the top of the page—extracts the form data from the request into local variables:

```
@{
    var title = Request["Title"];
    var summary = Request["Summary"];
    var body = Request["Body"];
}
```

The snippet uses the Request object as a dictionary, copying several values from the Request to local variables. Notice how the keys used to access the Request dictionary match those specified in the name field of each of the form's input fields. To prove that this works, add the following lines in the page's body, emitting the values from the Request:

```
@{
    var title = Request["Title"];
    var summary = Request["Summary"];
    var body = Request["Body"];
}

<fieldset>
    <legend>Posted Values: </legend>
```

```
<p>
    <label>Title: </label>
    <span>@title</span>
</p>

<p>
    <label>Summary: </label>
    <span>@summary</span>
</p>

<p><label>Body: </label></p>
<p><div>@body</div></p>

</fieldset>
```

With the above code in place, try to Run the page. Enter test data into the form fields, and then click Add Post. You should see the values you've entered rendered back at the top of the page.

Saving Data to the Database

After verifying that the form page can post back to itself and extract the form post data from the request, the next step is to save those values to the database. Luckily, Web-Matrix's database helper makes database access simple and straightforward. As the following example shows, it takes only a few lines and standard SQL to insert the values extracted from the request into a database table:

```
@{
    var title = Request["Title"];
    var summary = Request["Summary"];
    var body = Request["Body"];

    if(IsPost)
    {
        Database
            .Open("Blog")
            .Execute("INSERT INTO Posts (Title, Summary, Body) " +
                    "VALUES(@0,@1,@2)",
                    title, summary, body);
    }
}
```

The new section begins with a qualifier: since we are using the same page for both showing the form and saving the posted data to the database, the database call can only be made in reaction to a form post. Otherwise, this section should be skipped and the page displayed without inserting anything into the database. In order to determine whether or not the page is reacting to a form post, line 6 checks the page's IsPost property. When this value is false (i.e., the page is not reacting to a form post), the database logic will be skipped and the rest of the page shown as expected. When the page is reacting to a form post, however, this value will be true, and the database query will be executed.

Lines 8–12 (which are actually one statement spread over multiple lines) show the database query. The call to `Database.Open("Blog")` first opens a connection to the database, ready to accept queries. The `Database.Execute()` statement spanning lines 10–12 executes a standard SQL `INSERT` statement against this connection, injecting the form post values previously extracted from the `Request` object as numbered parameters.

As expected, the Posts table in WebMatrix's Database view (displayed in Figure 2-7) shows posted data inserted into the database.

Figure 2-7. Posted form data is visible in WebMatrix's Database view

Feel free to populate the database with more sample posts to prepare for the next step: displaying a list of posts on the home page.

Validating Posted Data

Accepting and storing invalid data can often be more detrimental than not accepting any data at all. On the Web, form posts are the primary way that data is exchanged between users and applications. Most data collected from users has some sort of requirements placed on it, validating that the data meets certain expectations before the application does anything with it. Validation can be as simple as requiring that a form field not be empty, that the field be a certain type, or that a value fall within a particular range. Since form validation is so ubiquitous, most mature web application frameworks offer some way to express and evaluate business rules against posted form data.

Conversion helpers

Before we begin writing code to validate our form post values, it is worth pointing out that WebMatrix offers a handful of helper methods that make the job of validating form field values simpler and more straightforward. They are broken into two groups: string conversion helpers and type verification helpers.

The methods `AsBool()`, `AsDateTime()`, `AsDecimal()`, `AsFloat()`, and `AsInt()` attempt to parse values of the respective type from `string` variables. Strings are the default type for all Request values. The statement `"42".AsInt()` would evaluate the `string` value `"42"` and parse the number to the `int` return value, `42`.

Each of these methods also includes an optional parameter to return in the event that parsing fails. For example, attempts to parse the string value `"word"` will fail, but if you provide a default value as a parameter to the `.AsInt()` method, it will return that value instead:

```
var intValue = "word".AsInt(10);  // returns the int value 10
```

The methods `IsBool()`, `IsDateTime()`, `IsDecimal()`, `IsFloat()`, and `IsInt()` can check the type of a value. It is often more effective to check that a value can be converted than to try (and fail) to convert the value. Preemptive conversion checks can help make logic significantly cleaner and easier to read. For instance:

```
if(Request["id"].IsInt())
```

is easier to understand than:

```
var id = Request["id"].IsInt(-1);  // Use -1 as a "magic number"
if(id != -1) { /* ... */ }+
```

While both of these approaches effectively lead to the same result, the first approach is much more direct and declarative. The second approach bases its conditional logic on "magic values," arbitrary values that affect processing but have no intrinsic meaning. For example, what happens if `Request["id"]` actually *is* -1? The first approach uses very direct and declarative language that explains exactly how the code behaves and reads almost like plain English.

Using validation

Razor views can make excellent use of the available helper methods to validate form post values and determine the best course of action to take. To show the validation in action, let's revisit the Add Post page example. As it stands, users can submit anything—and that includes nothing (a blank field)—into every form field. The database schema will not allow empty values in any of its fields, and if a user tries to submit an empty value, he or she will be greeted with an ugly database exception. That might serve to keep empty data out of the database, but it doesn't make for a very nice user experience!

To create a better user experience, it is best to check for invalid conditions *before* attempting to save to the database. That way, if the user attempts to post invalid data, he or she will be prompted with helpful messages indicating which fields are invalid and why. Armed with this knowledge, the user can correct the invalid fields and try to resubmit the form.

The following example shows the previous *AddPost.cshtml* view, updated to include some basic validation logic:

```
@{
    Layout = "~/_AdminLayout.cshtml";

    var title = Request["Title"];
    var summary = Request["Summary"];
    var body = Request["Body"];

    // Only validate form fields during a POST (not during the initial GET)
```

```
if(IsPost) {
    if(title.IsEmpty()) {
        ModelState.AddError("Title", "Post title cannot be empty");
    }

    if(summary.IsEmpty()) {
        ModelState.AddError("Summary", "Post summary cannot be empty");
    }

    if(body.IsEmpty()) {
        ModelState.AddError("Body", "Post body cannot be empty");
    }
}
}

@if (IsPost && ModelState.IsValid)
{
    Database
        .Open("Blog")
        .Execute("INSERT INTO Posts (Title, Summary, Body) " +
                "VALUES(@0,@1,@2)",
                title, summary, body);

    <fieldset>
        <legend>Posted Values: </legend>

        <p>
            <label>Title: </label>
            <span>@title</span>
        </p>

        <p>
            <label>Summary: </label>
            <span>@summary</span>
        </p>

        <p><label>Body: </label></p>
        <p><div>@body</div></p>

    </fieldset>
}

<form method="post" action="">
    <fieldset>

        <legend>New Blog Post</legend>

        @Html.ValidationSummary()

        <div>
            @Html.ValidationMessage("Title", "*")
            <label for="Title">Title</label>
            <input type="text" name="Title" value="@title"/>
        </div>
```

```
<div>
    @Html.ValidationMessage("Summary", "*")
    <label for="Summary">Summary</label>
    <input type="text" name="Summary" value="@summary" />
</div>

<div>
    <p>
        @Html.ValidationMessage("Body", "*")
        <label for="Body">Body</label>
    </p>
    <textarea cols="40" rows="10" name="Body">@body</textarea>
</div>

<div>
    <button type="submit">Add Post</button>
</div>

        </fieldset>
    </form>
```

There is quite a bit going on in this example!

The template starts out the same, specifying the Layout and reading the form post values from the Request object. After getting a copy of the form post values, we quickly dive into the validation logic. Each field gets validated; in this example, users can enter any value they like, as long as they enter *something* (i.e., the field is invalid if IsEmpty() returns true). When a field fails the check, add it to the special ModelState object, associated with a message to show the user that explains why the field is invalid. The errors tracked by the ModelState object drive the rest of the logic on the page. Since the validation errors (if any) are tracked in the ModelState object, it is easy to check if the form post data as a whole is valid by looking at the ModelState.IsValid property. If no errors occurred, the ModelState.IsValid property will reflect this by returning false.

The ModelState.IsValid property can be called throughout the template as many times as needed, making it very easy to change how the page renders when validation errors occur. The first code affected by whether or not the posted data is valid is the decision to execute the SQL statement that saves the values to the database. In other words, only save the posted data to the database when it is valid: that is the whole reason for validation logic! Included in this block is the summary markup showing the values that were saved to the database. The summary is included within the conditional block because it should only show after the data has been successfully saved to the database.

The main content of the page immediately follows the database logic and summary. The important part that's been added here is the call to the @Html.ValidationSummary() method—a helper method that displays a list of any errors that were added to the ModelState object earlier in the page. The summary section only shows when the ModelState object contains validation errors. Otherwise, no markup regarding validation renders. When there are validation errors in a page, the `@Html.ValidationSum` `mary()` method renders the errors as an HTML list:

```
<div class="validation-summary-errors">
    <ul>
        <li>Post title cannot be empty</li>
        <li>Post summary cannot be empty</li>
        <li>Post body cannot be empty</li>
    </ul>
</div>
```

With no CSS styles applied to it, the list of errors will appear just like any other `<ul>` on the page. But this list is much more important than those `<ul>`s—it needs to grab the user's attention and tell him there were errors in the form he tried to submit! Luckily, the `@Html.ValidationSummary()` helper adds the `validation-summary-errors` CSS class by default. With the `validation-summary-errors` CSS class in place, you can easily write CSS styles that target the list and format it to your liking. Make the text bolder, make it larger, change the color to red…whatever you think will grab the user's attention.

Finally, the remainder of the template remains largely untouched, except for calls to the `@Html.ValidationMessage()` helper added before every field label, which looks like this:

```
@Html.ValidationMessage("Title")
```

The `@Html.ValidationMessage()` helper can be applied to any field that might fail validation. The helper checks the `ModelState` object to see if a validation error has been registered for the field name specified by the first parameter of the `@Html.Validation` `Message()` method call (in this example, the `"Title"` field). If so, the helper emits markup indicating to the user that the field is invalid and needs to be corrected. By default, the helper includes the error message that was originally associated with the field when the `ModelState.AddError()` call was made; however, you can override the contents of the inline validation message by adding a second parameter to the `@Html.ValidationMes` `sage()` method call containing the alternative content to display. Here's what the previous example looks like with a custom validation message (the * character) specified:

```
@Html.ValidationMessage("Title", "*")
```

Using this markup, if there is an error associated with the `"Title"` field in the `Model` `State` object, the following markup will be rendered to the user:

```
<span class="field-validation-error">*</span>
```

Here again, as with the `@Html.ValidationSummary()` helper, the `@Html.ValidationMes` `sage()` helper attaches a CSS class (`field-validation-error`) to the span that it renders so that you or your designers can leverage CSS styles to call attention to the validation error.

Creating the Home Page

The home page is the first page that most visitors will see. As such, it should be as interesting as possible to encourage visitors to explore more of the site. On a blog, the home page generally contains a list of the most recent posts, along with links to the RSS feed, social media, etc. The following section demonstrates how to use the Database helper to retrieve and display the blog posts entered using the form from the previous section.

After using the Database.Execute() method to insert data into the database using standard SQL statements, it should be no surprise to find out that the Database.Query() method allows you to retrieve data, also using standard SQL statements. The code and markup will look similar to that used for the Add Post page. The following example shows the page in its entirety:

```
@{
    var db = Database.Open("Blog");
    var posts = db.Query("SELECT ID,Title,Body FROM Posts");
}

<!DOCTYPE html>

<html lang="en">
    <head>
        <meta charset="utf-8" />
        <title>My Blog</title>
    </head>
    <body>

    <h1>My Blog</h1>

    @foreach(var post in posts) {
        <div>
            <h3>@post.Title</h3>
            <div>@post.Body</div>
        </div>
    }

</body>
</html>
```

Just as in the previous section, the page starts, on line 2, by opening a connection to the Blog database that stores the posts. Line 3 executes a standard SQL statement, retrieving the ID, Title, and Body columns from the Posts table and storing them in a local variable. Later, a foreach statement iterates through the posts, pulling each one into a local post variable. This loop begins with an opening bracket and ends with the closing bracket after the <div> tag that it wraps.

These brackets contain a combination of code and markup which—when iterated over in the foreach loop—produces a list of blog posts. Each post will be wrapped in a

`<div>` tag and contains the post's Title in an `<h3>` tag and the post's Body in its own `<div>` tag. When this page executes, it produces this HTML:

```html
<html lang="en">
    <head>
        <meta charset="utf-8" />
        <title>My Blog</title>
    </head>
    <body>

    <h1>My Blog</h1>

        <div>
            <h3>Test Post #1</h3>
            <div>This is the first test post</div>
        </div>

        <div>
            <h3>Test Post #2</h3>
            <div>This is the second test post</div>
        </div>

        <div>
            <h3>Test Post #3</h3>
            <div>This is the third test post</div>
        </div>

    </body>
</html>
```

CHAPTER 3

Organizing Razor Templates

As the size of a website grows, so does the task of keeping everything organized. And, as any seasoned web developer will tell you: the bigger your site, the more difficult it becomes to maintain. Luckily, there are plenty of techniques developers can employ to keep websites from growing unmanageable. This chapter will introduce a number of Razor features that help make website organization and management a breeze.

Layouts

Now that our blog site has more than one page, you can begin to see that there is a bit of redundant markup between them. It is generally a good thing for all pages on your website to look the same; that is, they should look like they belong to the same site.

Thus far, the pages have maintained a consistent look and feel by duplicating the same markup on every new page, changing only the main content section. Not only is duplicating text in this way inefficient, it quickly becomes practically impossible to manage. For example, consider how much work it would take to add a simple CSS stylesheet to a site with a dozen or more individually maintained pages.

The problem of maintaining a consistent look and feel throughout an entire website is certainly not limited to WebMatrix and ASP.NET MVC sites. In fact, all good web frameworks must address this problem. Most address it by introducing the concept of a "layout." When using layouts, a single page acts as a template for all other pages to use, defining the site-wide page layout and style.

A layout template typically includes the main markup (scripts, CSS stylesheets, and structural HTML elements, such as navigation and content containers), specifying locations within the markup in which pages can define content. Each page in the site refers to this layout, including only the content within the locations the layout has indicated.

Take a look at a typical Razor layout file (_Layout.cshtml_):

```
<!DOCTYPE html>

<html lang="en">
    <head>
        <meta charset="utf-8" />
        <title>@View.Title</title>
    </head>
    <body>
        <div class="header">
            @RenderSection("Header")
        </div>

        @RenderBody()

        <div class="footer">
            @RenderSection("Footer")
        </div>
    </body>
</html>
```

The layout file contains the main HTML content, defining the HTML structure for the entire site. The layout relies on variables (such as `@View.Title`) and special functions like `@RenderSection([Section Name])` and `@RenderBody()` to interact with individual pages.

Once a Razor layout is defined, pages reference the layout and supply content for the sections defined within the layout. The following is a basic content page that refers to the previously defined _Layout.cshtml_ file:

```
@{ Layout = "~/_Layout.cshtml"; }

@section Header {
    <h1>My Blog<h1>
}

@section Footer {
    Copyright 2011
}

<div class="main">
    This is the main content.
</div>
```

Figure 3-1 shows the HTML that would be rendered from the HTML above. The figure has been color-coded to help you better visualize which content comes from the layout and which content comes from the page.

Like puzzle pieces, Razor layouts and the content pages that depend on them work together, each one defining portions of the entire page. When all the pieces get assembled, the result is a complete web page.

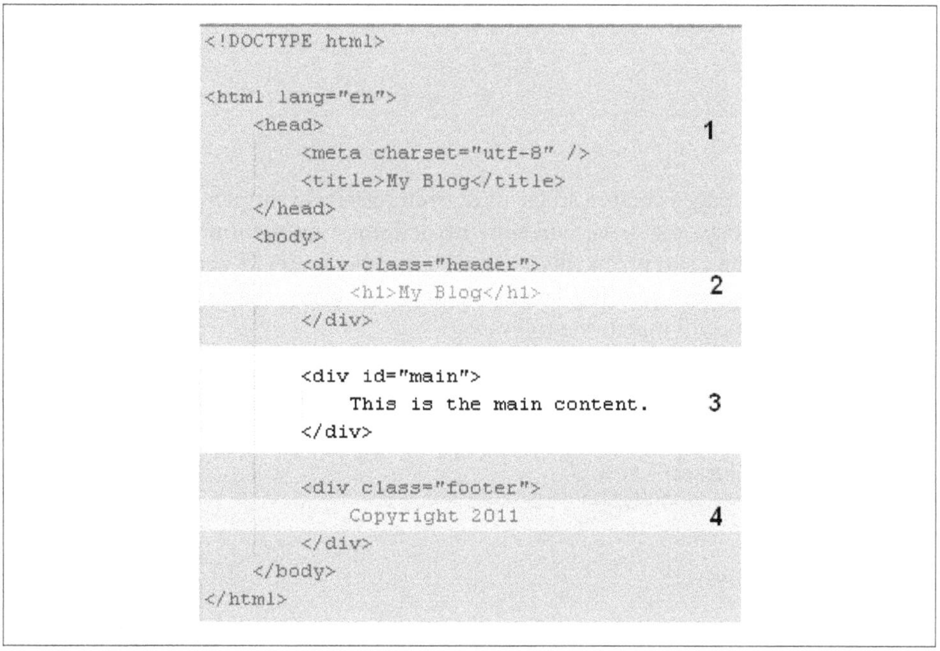

```
<!DOCTYPE html>

<html lang="en">
    <head>
        <meta charset="utf-8" />                    1
        <title>My Blog</title>
    </head>
    <body>
        <div class="header">
            <h1>My Blog</h1>                         2
        </div>

        <div id="main">
            This is the main content.               3
        </div>

        <div class="footer">
            Copyright 2011                           4
        </div>
    </body>
</html>
```

Figure 3-1. HTML with color coding to indicate layout sections

Layouts Are Pages, Too!

Not only does Razor support the concept of layouts, but Razor layouts are also incredibly easy to define and use. Razor uses a master layout file and each page refers to this master layout. The master layout file is just a Razor template (*.cshtml* or *.vbhtml* file) that includes specific keywords to indicate which portions of the template the individual pages will replace. To show Razor layouts in action, we will update the example blog site, adding a new layout template and updating the two existing pages to leverage this template.

The first step in introducing a new layout is to create a new Razor template file. To add this file, right-click on the Empty Site folder and select "New File." Then select the CSHTML file type (just as we have been doing for the other pages) and name it *_Layout.cshtml*.

The contents of the resulting file (shown below) should not be surprising, as they are the same template that each of the other CSHTML files in our project has started with. The difference with this file is that, instead of adding content directly to it, we will add Razor code to define sections that other pages will refer to!

```
<!DOCTYPE html>

<html lang="en">
    <head>
        <meta charset="utf-8" />
```

```
        <title></title>
    </head>
    <body>

    </body>
</html>
```

Since the example pages created so far have been relatively simple—only adding content within the <body> tag— we will start by defining one section: the main content body. Assuming the contents of this section should be rendered within the <body> tag (with no additional surrounding layout elements or CSS), the master layout Razor template's contents will match the following:

```
<!DOCTYPE html>

<html lang="en">
    <head>
        <meta charset="utf-8" />
        <title>My Blog</title>
    </head>
    <body>
        @RenderBody()
    </body>
</html>
```

Notice that the only difference between the default contents and the layout template is the page title and the addition of a single method call: @RenderBody(). This command renders the output of the executed content view at the same point at which the Render Body() command is called (line 9 in this case). All Razor layouts must include a call to the RenderBody() method at some point in their content.

Once the layout is defined, any Razor template may leverage the layout by specifying the layout's file location in the Razor template's Layout property. What follows is a modified version of the example blog site's *Default.cshtml* page, pointing the Layout property to *_Layout.cshtml* and removing all of the redundant lines. The result of this exercise is that *Default.cshtml* is now much smaller and more focused, defining only the logic and contents pertinent to displaying this particular page and a pointer to the desired layout instead of repeating the site's layout markup. Now *Default.cshtml* can concentrate on its specific logic and markup and let the layout page worry about the site layout!

```
@{
    Layout = "~/_Layout.cshtml";
    var db = Database.Open("Blog");
    var posts = db.Query("SELECT ID,Title,Body FROM Posts");
}

<h1>My Blog</h1>

@foreach(var post in posts) {
    <div>
        <h3>@post.Title</h3>
```

```
        <div>@post.Body</div>
    </div>
}
```

Sections

Though the RenderBody() command is very useful in allowing content pages to specify what content should appear within a master page, typically just the simplest layouts will have only one dynamic section that needs to be replaced. To this end, developers can use the RenderSection() command to specify sections of the layout template in which content pages may render additional dynamic content. The next snippet updates the previous layout example to include two new header and footer sections:

```
<!DOCTYPE html>

<html lang="en">
    <head>
        <meta charset="utf-8" />
        <title>My Blog</title>
    </head>
    <body>
        <div class="header">
            @RenderSection("Header")
        </div>

        @RenderBody()

        <div class="footer">
            @RenderSection("Footer", required: false)
        </div>
    </body>
</html>
```

The RenderSection() call includes an additional parameter—"required"—indicating whether or not content pages following this layout are required to explicitly implement a given section. This value is true by default (indicating that content pages are required to implement a given section); however, if this value is false, content pages can feel free to ignore that the section is defined, providing content for the optional section only when prudent. Content pages then refer to these dynamic sections using the Razor section keyword, with this syntax:

```
@section [Section Name] {
    [ Razor content, code, and markup ]
}
```

The following snippet updates the blog site's home page (*Default.cshtml*) to include content for a Header section, but has opted not to define content for the optional Footer section by simply omitting a second @section area. Though shown near the top of the template in this example, section definitions may appear almost anywhere within the Razor template and need not be constrained to the top of the template before the main template content:

```
@{
    Layout = "~/_Layout.cshtml";
    var db = Database.Open("Blog");
    var posts = db.Query("SELECT ID,Title,Body FROM Posts");
}

@section Header {
    <h1>My Blog</h1>
}

    @foreach(var post in posts) {
        <div>
            <h3>@post.Title</h3>
            <div>@post.Body</div>
        </div>
    }
```

IsSectionDefined

Razor also provides another helpful method—IsSectionDefined()—which determines whether a section of a given name is defined in the content view. This information allows the layout not only to control the placement of the section's content but also to affect other areas of the page.

Consider the Footer section example above, in which the section content is wrapped in a containing div element. What if you wanted the view to omit the containing div entirely when a content view does not provide content for the optional Footer section (it is, after all, an optional section)? Luckily, the IsSectionDefined() method makes this a trivial task:

```
@RenderBody()

@if(IsSectionDefined("Footer")) {
    <div class="footer">
        @RenderSection("Footer", required: false)
    </div>
}
</body>
</html>
```

With this check in place, the footer div will only be rendered when the content view defines a Footer section. Otherwise, nothing will be rendered!

Nested Layouts

Layouts can also be "nested." A nested layout is any layout that refers to another, outer layout. This approach is useful when a subset of pages require the same markup, as is often the case when certain sections of a website need to appear slightly different from the others, yet retain the same general look and feel.

Since it provides functionality that only certain people will use, the Add Post (*Add-Post.cshtml*) page created in Chapter 2 is a prime candidate for a nested layout. Applying a nested layout to the Add Post page will allow it to use the same overall theme as the rest of the site (the *_Layout.cshtml* layout), yet slightly alter its color scheme to indicate that the page belongs to an administrative area.

When we first created it, the Add Post page used the default CSHTML file template, which does not refer to a layout at all. Thus, the first step to applying a nested layout to the Add Post page is to remove everything but its core content (everything inside the <body> tag). After this, use the same syntax as earlier examples to associate the page with a layout, only instead of the *_Layout.cshtml* layout specify another (not yet created) layout file named *~/_AdminLayout.cshtml*. The first few lines of the modified page are shown below:

```
@{
    Layout = "~/_AdminLayout.cshtml";

    var title = Request["Title"];
    var summary = Request["Summary"];
    var body = Request["Body"];
        ...
}
```

Now it's time to create the aforementioned *_AdminLayout.cshtml* layout. To do so, add a new CSHTML file named *_AdminLayout.cshtml* to the root of the website (follow the same steps used previously to create a new layout file). Then, completely clear the default template text, so that the file is empty, and replace with a reference to the *_Layout.cshtml* layout file as well as a call to the RenderBody() method. The following snippet shows the full implementation of a nested layout: a Razor template that contains a call to the RenderBody() method and refers to another layout:

```
@{ Layout = "_Layout.cshtml"; }
@RenderBody()
```

Nested Layouts and Sections

Technically speaking, the above code is all that is required to implement a nested layout. However, if you attempt to execute the site with only this code in place, you will quickly find out that the original layout—*_Layout.cshtml*—is not satisfied: *_AdminLayout.cshtml* does not implement the required Header section!

As shown earlier, a content view can define Razor sections that the view's layout can access and execute. These section definitions, however, are only accessible to the immediate layout and vice-versa. In the case of the Add Post → Admin Layout → Main Site Layout scenario, this means that only the admin layout can access any sections defined in the Add Post content view. The main site layout cannot interact with the Add Post content view at all! Conversely, the admin layout is responsible for implementing the required sections that the main site layout expects—it must explicitly implement these sections and cannot simply pass this responsibility to the Add Post content view.

Redefining Sections

Though this may seem inconvenient at first, consider what a Razor layout actually represents. At their core, layouts are nothing more than fancy Razor views that leverage a few special methods (RenderBody, RenderSection, etc.) to access content from the content views that refer to them. Thus, nested views are unique not only because they wrap a content view by referring to another layout, but also because they act as a content view themselves. If you take this into consideration, this layered approach makes much more sense: each layer must satisfy the layer above it.

What this all means is that each layer is able to redefine what is required of the content views that will leverage it. Though nested views must implement the sections expected of layouts higher up the chain, they can also modify how—or if—those sections are handled by their content views.

Let's revisit the nested admin layout example. The main site layout refers to two sections—Header and Footer—but allows one of the sections (the Footer section) to remain undefined. Thus, in order to get the admin layout working, it must define a Header section. The updated _AdminLayout.cshtml page contains the bare minimum required to satisfy the main site layout's expectations:

```
@{ Layout = "_Layout.cshtml"; }

@section Header {  /* EMPTY! */ }

@RenderBody()
```

With the Header section definition in place, the Add Post page now executes (hooray!). However, what if the Add Post page would like to render something in the Header section defined in the main site layout? It can't! At least not directly...

Though sections may only be defined by the immediate view (the nested layout), there is nothing stopping the nested layout from turning around and requesting a section of the same name from its immediate views. Here's the updated _AdminLayout.cshtml, which effectively redefines the Header section for its content views:

```
@{ Layout = "_Layout.cshtml"; }

@section Header {
    @RenderSection("Header", required: false)
}

@RenderBody()
```

Notice that, instead of simply passing on the requirement to implement the Header section, the nested admin layout effectively "converts" it to an optional section by specifying that it is not required (required: false).

The Layout Rendering Life Cycle

While it's nice to know that Razor layouts render HTML as developers intend, it is useful to know just how they go about doing so. At first glance, you might assume that the Razor executes in the same order that it gets rendered in, but this is not actually the case.

Figure 3-2 shows the blog layout we've been creating in this chapter split into color-coded sections, numbered with the order in which they are rendered to the user.

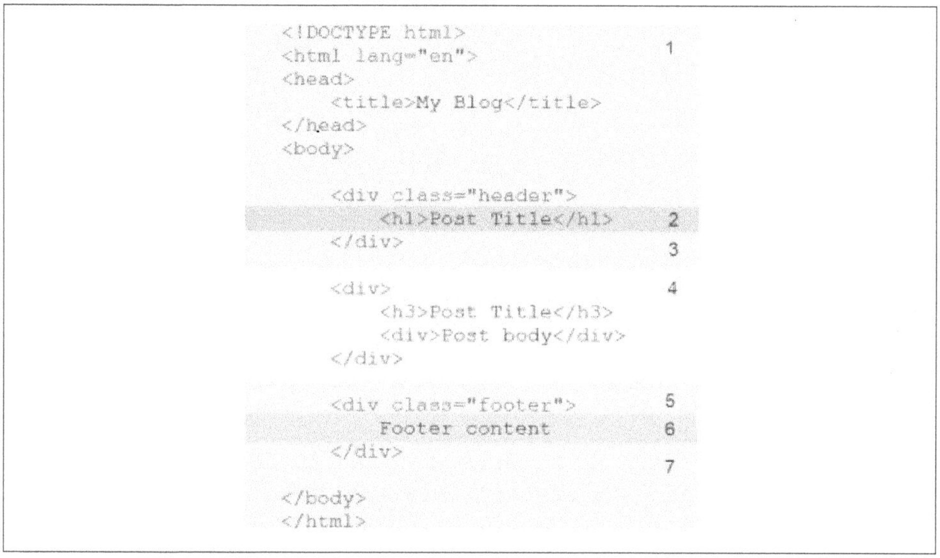

```
<!DOCTYPE html>
<html lang="en">                          1
<head>
    <title>My Blog</title>
</head>
<body>

    <div class="header">
            <h1>Post Title</h1>      2
    </div>                            3

    <div>                             4
        <h3>Post Title</h3>
        <div>Post body</div>
    </div>

    <div class="footer">             5
        Footer content               6
    </div>
                                      7

</body>
</html>
```

Figure 3-2. A page showing the order in which blocks are rendered

As shown, the numbered sections correspond to the following files:

1. *_Layout.cshtml*
2. The Header section in *Post.cshtml*
3. *_Layout.cshtml*
4. The body of *Post.cshtml*
5. *_Layout.cshtml*
6. The Footer section in *Post.cshtml*
7. *_Layout.cshtml*

Though this may be the order that they are rendered, this is not actually the order in which they are executed on the server (see Figure 3-3).

Though this order of execution may be surprising at first, it provides a very telling glimpse under the hood of the Razor engine. Take a moment to consider the actual web

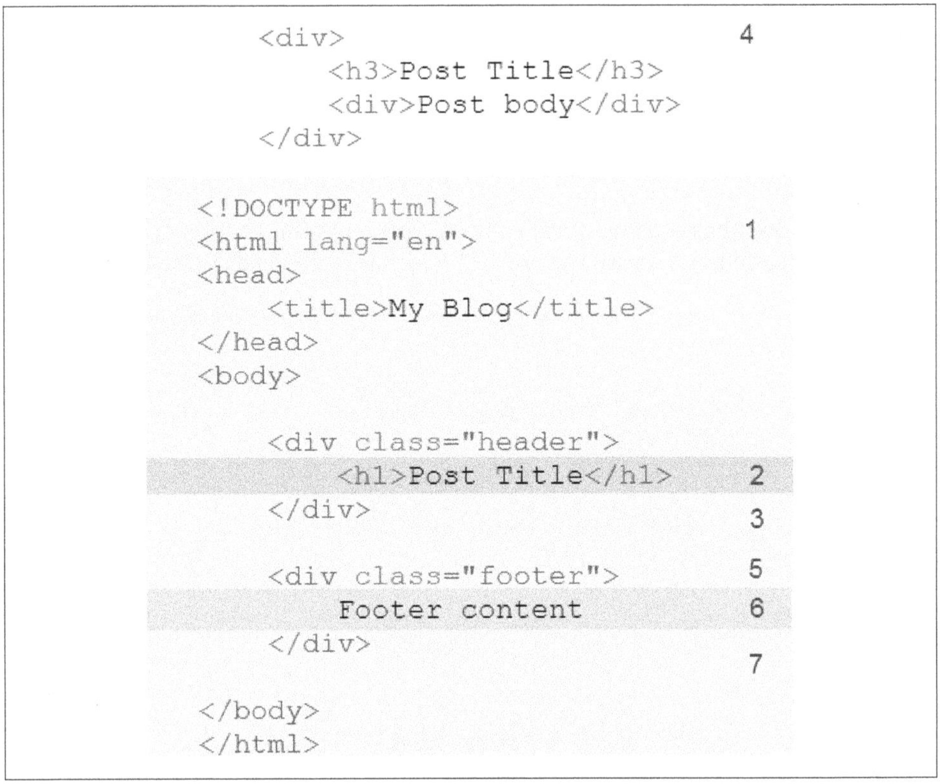

```
    <div>                               4
        <h3>Post Title</h3>
        <div>Post body</div>
    </div>


<!DOCTYPE html>
<html lang="en">                        1
<head>
    <title>My Blog</title>
</head>
<body>

    <div class="header">
        <h1>Post Title</h1>            2
    </div>                              3

    <div class="footer">               5
        Footer content                 6
    </div>
                                       7

</body>
</html>
```

Figure 3-3. The parts of a Razor view, displayed in order of execution

request made by the user—it is a request to the *Post.cshtml* page. As such, it is only natural that the body of this page be the first to execute.

Had *Post.cshtml* not specified a layout, Razor would have gladly rendered only the output of this page and stopped there. However, since it does reference a layout, *Post.cshtml* passes control to the specified layout view after executing itself. The layout is able to control content placement using the RenderBody() method shown earlier to access the output of the already-executed *Post.cshtml* (or any other view referenced in this manner).

Next, look at where sections 2 and 6—the Header and Footer sections—are located in the rendering life cycle. As discussed earlier in the book, Razor sections are blocks of code that may be defined in views for later use by a layout. While layouts are able to access sections, the page-specific code in these sections is not executed along with the main body. Razor sections are, in fact, effectively functions (lambda expressions, to be exact) that are simply defined in views, but only executed when explicitly invoked from a layout.

Nested Layouts

Now that you have a strong grasp of the Razor layout life cycle, it's time to throw a wrench into the mix: how do nested layouts affect the rendering order? The answer:

1. Content view
2. Nested layout
3. Wrapper (main) layout

Previous sections demonstrated that Razor views that leverage layouts render the content view first, followed by the layout (which injects the output from the content view). Since nested layouts effectively act as both layouts and content views, they simply add another layer to the mix. Thus, the requested content view is rendered first, which passes its output to the nested layout, which subsequently wraps the original content view with itself, and then passes its output to the final main layout.

Partial Views

Layouts and sections are a powerful and effective technique for creating maintainable websites because they provide the ability to split a given web page into smaller, more focused parts. In addition to layouts and sections, WebMatrix offers yet another compartmentalization technique called *partial views*, which are self-contained portions of markup that can be reused throughout the website. Partial views are also useful for separating complex or lengthy portions of markup from a page, making them easier to read and understand (and by extension, easier to maintain).

Creating Partial Views

To create a partial view, it is often easiest to start with existing markup from an existing web page. For example, assume that we'd like to create a new page to show the contents of a single blog post, reusing the markup within the `foreach` loop on the blog's home page that lists all of the blog posts:

```
@foreach(var in posts) {
    var url = "http://www.myblog.com/posts/post.cshtml"id=" + post.ID;

    <div>
        <h3>@post.Title</h3>
        <div>@post.Body</div>
        @TwitterHelpers.TweetButton( url: url, text: @post.Title )
        @Facebook.LikeButton( href: url )
    </div>
}
```

In order to turn the inner contents of the `foreach` loop into a partial view, you must first create a new Razor file to hold the contents of the new partial view. To do so, right-click on the Posts folder and from the New File dialog, select the CSHTML file type (that's right, the same file type we've been using for full Razor pages and layouts). Name the new file *_Posts.cshtml*, and then cut lines 12 through 19 from the *Default.cshtml* file and paste them into this new view, overwriting the existing contents completely. Then, replace the contents of the **foreach** loop with a single line—a call to the **Render Page()** method, passing in the relative path of the new partial view file, along with any parameters the partial view expects (which will be explained in a bit), like so:

```
RenderPage("Posts/_Post.cshtml", new { Post = post })
```

Here's the entire contents of the updated *Default.cshtml*:

```
@{
    Layout = "~/_Layout.cshtml";
    var db = Database.Open("Blog");
    var posts = db.Query("SELECT ID,Title,Body FROM Posts");
}

@section Header {
    <h1>My Blog</h1>
}

@foreach(var post in posts) {
    @RenderPage("~/Posts/_Post.cshtml", new { Post = post })
}
```

And the new *_Posts.cshtml* file:

```
@{
    var post = Page.Post;
    var url = "http://www.myblog.com/posts/post.cshtml"id=" + post.ID;
}

<div>
    <h3>@post.Title</h3>
    <div>@post.Body</div>
    @TwitterHelpers.TweetButton( url: url, text: @post.Title )
    @Facebook.LikeButton( href: url )
</div>
```

Accessing parameter values

For partial views with simple markup, these steps are all that is required. However, since the markup we chose to turn into a partial view contains references to an object (the **post** variable), the partial view must first gain access to a local reference of that variable. To see where the value of this variable originates, refer back to line 12 of the updated *Default.cshtml* markup, which passed **new { Post = post }** as the second parameter to the **RenderPage** method. The partial view is able to access the values in this second parameter via the **Page** object, like so:

```
var post = Page.Post;
```

Once created, this local reference satisfies the references to the post variable in the copied code. With the post variable reference in place, you should be able to execute

---

the *Default.cshtml* page and see that it renders the same markup as before the move to partial views; only now, that markup lives in a separate file!

Alternatively, the `RenderPage()` method accepts any number of parameters in lieu of a single object. If we chose to use this approach, *Default.cshtml* would contain the following:

```
@RenderPage("Posts/_Post.cshtml", post)
```

The `post` variable reference in the *_Post.cshtml* partial view could still be created, this time using the `PageData` object's index accessor, like so:

```
var post = PageData[1];
```

Though this approach may be quite effective in many situations, it—like all index-based techniques—relies on the relatively arbitrary order in which the parameters are passed. Should this order change, all calls to the partial view would need to be updated, which may involve updating multiple locations. Conversely, the named approach shown earlier refers to the parameters by name, regardless of the order in which they are defined. Though these names are case-sensitive and also somewhat arbitrary, they provide much more semantic meaning than numerical index values. The named approach is, therefore, often much easier to update and maintain and is the author's recommended approach.

Reusing Partial Views

It's understandable if you were unimpressed by the result of the previous exercise in moving markup from a web page to a partial view. The real power of partial views is best shown when a partial view is used in more than one place. To this end, we will now create an additional page that will refer to the same partial view, therefore leveraging the same markup in multiple pages.

You may have noticed that the previous examples have been referring to the generated URL *http://www.myblog.com/posts/post.cshtml"id=@post.ID* and that this tutorial has not yet created a page named *Post.cshtml* in the Posts folder of the example website. If that is the case, you are exactly right—so let's create it now, using the new partial view.

As opposed to the home page, which lists all of the blog posts, the new page—*/Posts/Post.cshtml*—will show only one, making it easy for visitors and search engines to link to a single post on the blog. What's more, if you've read the previous few sections, the contents of this new page will be no surprise.

First, begin by creating a new CSHTML page under the Posts folder named *Post.cshtml*. Next, begin the page with a code snippet that retrieves the requested post from the database. Finally, pass the blog post retrieved from the database into the `RenderPage` method, just as shown previously. Take a look at the full contents of the new *Post.cshtml* file with these changes in place:

```
@{
    Layout = "~/_Layout.cshtml";
    var db = Database.Open("Blog");
    var post = db.QuerySingle("SELECT ID,Title,Body FROM Posts WHERE ID = @0",
                              Request["id"]);
}

@section Header {
    <h1>@post.Title</h1>
}

@RenderPage("_Post.cshtml", new { Post = post })
```

 The _ prefix applied to partial views is more than just a helpful indicator to help differentiate partial views from full pages; it also offers a bit of security. As far as IIS is concerned, any Razor view with the _ prefix is not meant to be viewed by itself, so IIS will reject any direct requests for files with the _ applied to them.

Though the partial view code in this example should not come as a surprise, the snippet does include a few things that we have not yet covered. Specifically:

1. Since the page requires and requests only one **post** object from the database, line 4 uses the **QuerySingle** method instead of the **Query** method used in earlier examples. As expected, this method returns a single object instead of a list of objects.

2. The SQL query later on the same line (line 4) leverages a parameterized SQL string to help sanitize inputs and protect against SQL injection attacks. This is a standard best practice as opposed to the use of "dynamic SQL" (using string concatenation to build SQL query strings).

3. The page determines which post the user wants to view by examining the request to find the post's ID value. It does this in line 5 by requesting the value of the "**id**" key from the page's **Request** dictionary object, which contains the values of variables from multiple aspects of the request, including its query string and/or form **post** data.

At this point, we have created a pretty functional website. The site provides the ability to add new content and then display that content to users. What's more, the pages leverage Razor layouts and sections to maintain a consistent theme across pages, making it easier to edit and maintain a centralized look and feel throughout the site. The next section will take our "functional" site to the next level, using Razor Helpers to enhance the site and provide users with a better experience.

Razor Helpers

Razor Helpers provide an easy way to define common Razor markup in one centralized location and reuse that markup across your site. You can think of them much like global methods, except that Razor markup offers the ability to mix code and HTML markup rather than containing just code. Luckily, creating and using Razor Helpers is very simple and straightforward.

The easiest way to begin writing a Razor Helper is to choose an existing Razor page in your site, and then write and test the Razor markup that you wish to reuse. To demonstrate, let's modify the blog site's Post markup, adding a link to the template for each of the blog posts that allows visitors to share a direct link to the post via Twitter. The HTML for creating this button, as copied from Twitter's developer website, is as follows:

```
<script src="http://platform.twitter.com/widgets.js" type="text/javascript"></script>
<div>
    <a href="http://twitter.com/share" class="twitter-share-button"
        data-url="http://dev.twitter.com/pages/tweet_button"
        data-text="Checking out this page about Tweet Buttons">Tweet</a>
</div>
```

After inserting the Twitter markup, the _Post.cshtml partial view looks like this:

```
@{
    var post = Page.Post;
    var url = "http://www.myblog.com/posts/post.cshtml?id=" + post.ID;
}

<div>
    <h3>@post.Title</h3>
    <div>@post.Body</div>
    <script src="http://platform.twitter.com/widgets.js" type="text/javascript"></
script>
    <div>
        <a href="http://twitter.com/share" class="twitter-share-button"
            data-url="@url" data-text="@post.Title">Tweet</a>
    </div>
</div>
```

Note that the data-url and data-text portions of the anchor tag now contain the URL for this specific post and the post's title, respectively. With this information in place, this button will prompt the user with a pop-up window (shown in Figure 3-4), providing him or her the option to post the link and message to a Twitter account.

Figure 3-4. The TweetButton helper in action

So far, there is nothing particularly special about this code: it simply takes the Twitter template and adds a bit of Razor markup to insert details about the current blog post. The next step is to move this code into a Razor Helper function:

```
@helper TweetButton(string url, string text) {
    <script src="http://platform.twitter.com/widgets.js" type="text/javascript"></
script>
    <div>
        <a href="http://twitter.com/share" class="twitter-share-button"
           data-url="@url" data-text="@text">Tweet</a>
    </div>
}

@{
    var post = Page.Post;
    var url = "http://www.myblog.com/posts/post.cshtml?id=" + post.ID;
}

<div>
    <h3>@post.Title</h3>
    <div>@post.Body</div>
    @TweetButton(url: url, text: post.Title)
</div>
```

The newly created Razor Helper is defined in lines 11–17. The syntax is simple:

```
@helper [name] ( [parameters] ) {
    [Razor markup]
}
```

The @helper syntax effectively creates a static method behind the scenes, ready to be consumed throughout the rest of the page (or site!). Note that the "hardcoded" URL and text have been replaced with method parameters. This allows consumers of the helper to easily define its behavior without having to know the specifics of the HTML the helper generates. Lines 23–26 show an example of this helper in action with a simple call to the newly created TweetButton static method, passing in the post's URL and title.

The final step in the process of converting a Razor snippet into a global Razor Helper method that can be used across the entire site is to move the method into a location that is accessible by the whole site. Luckily, WebMatrix provides a special folder for just this purpose. If your site does not have this folder already, simply create a new folder in the root directory of the site named *App_Code*. In this folder, create a new CSHTML file named *TwitterHelpers.cshtml*, and then cut and paste the entire @helper method into this file, replacing any existing contents in the new file, as shown in the following TweetButton Helper Method:

```
@helper TweetButton(string url, string text) {
    <script src="http://platform.twitter.com/widgets.js" type="text/javascript"></
script>
    <div>
        <a href="http://twitter.com/share" class="twitter-share-button"
            data-url="@url" data-text="'@text'">Tweet</a>
    </div>
}
```

Once this is done, your site layout will look like that shown in Figure 3-5.

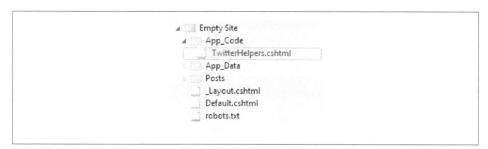

Figure 3-5. Website with TwitterHelpers.cshtml

Finally—since the Razor Helper has moved locations—update the @TweetButton reference to include the name of the new file. In our example, the updated markup will resemble the following:

```
<div>
    <h3>@post.Title</h3>
    <div>@post.Body</div>
    @TwitterHelpers.TweetButton( url: url, text: post.Title )
</div>
```

And that's all it takes—you have now created your first Razor Helper!

Razor Helper Packages

The Twitter Razor Helper demonstrated in this chapter is not very unique. In fact, it was largely code copied and pasted directly from the Internet. Though it is nice that Twitter provides code snippets that can be easily copied and pasted, it would be even nicer if we didn't have to create the Razor Helper ourselves at all. Luckily, we don't have to: WebMatrix websites have full access to an online repository containing potentially thousands of prebuilt packages, ready to install!

To install Razor Helpers from this online repository, start by navigating to your site's administration portal. The portal's Package Manager section should display a list of packages ready to be installed. Installation is as easy as choosing the package you want and clicking the Install button. The package is then downloaded and added to your website, ready for consumption.

For example, let's add Facebook integration in addition to the custom Twitter Helper previously created. To do this, search for "Facebook" with the Package Manager's search functionality, and then install the Facebook.Helper package. After installing, you should see a new file named *Facebook.cshtml* in the website's *App_Code* folder (the same place as the previously created *TwitterHelpers.cshtml*). Open this file and peruse it; you will see that it defines numerous functions and Razor Helpers. (The code is also very well documented and provides great sample code to learn from!)

Accessing the new Helpers defined in *Facebook.cshtml* is exactly the same as the previous examples with the custom Helper defined in *TwitterHelpers.cshtml*. The next code snippet leverages the Facebook.LikeButton Helper in addition to the TweetButton added previously, allowing visitors to share links to posts via Twitter or Facebook:

```
<div>
    <h3>@post.Title</h3>
    <div>@post.Body</div>
    @TwitterHelpers.TweetButton( url: url, text: post.Title )
    @Facebook.LikeButton( href: url )
</div>
```

Razor Helpers versus Partial Views

You might be thinking that the functionality offered by Razor Helpers seems awfully redundant with the partial view functionality discussed in the previous section. Though you are right in that they both provide a convenient way to share and reuse markup, sometimes it is more appropriate to use one over the other.

Razor Helpers

A Razor Helper is defined as a function with a specific set of input parameters that outputs rendered markup. Razor Helpers are most suitable for helping customize small sections of markup with minimal logic, such as an anchor tag or image tag. Since they typically contain less application-specific logic, they can often be used not only across views within the same project but also shared between applications. Think of Razor Helpers as templates or "macros" that make your code easier to read, write, and maintain.

Partial Views

Whereas Razor Helpers are best suited for small, generalized sections of markup, partial views are best for breaking up larger views into more manageable pieces. These pieces typically contain more application-specific markup and logic. Though partial views can be reused across views in a project, the application-specific logic present in most views generally precludes sharing across applications.

Conversely, just because it is possible to reuse a partial view in more than one place doesn't mean you have to. Partial views can be a very effective tool for simplifying a larger view or isolating a particularly complex section of a page. Do not shy away from creating a partial view because it will only be used in one place—not only is that OK, it's sometimes very helpful!

Executing Common Code

Web applications often have cross-cutting concerns. That is, there are site-wide activities and behaviors that affect some or all pages, regardless of what they have in common. Website activity logging is one of the classic examples: every page of the application triggers a log entry, despite the potentially vast differences between those pages.

Razor offers two ways to apply cross-cutting logic to your web application, both the first request for each individual page and before and after subsequent page requests.

Executing Code the First Time a Page Executes

Razor makes it very easy to execute code during the website's start-up phase. It does so via a special file in the website's root folder named _AppStart.cshtml, which gets executed only once during the application's lifetime, before the very first request. This is helpful for executing logic that should only ever be executed once per view, such as setting global variable values or initializing certain components.

As its file extension implies, _AppStart.cshtml is a Razor template like any other, so it must contain valid Razor markup. Outside of that constraint, you are free to do whatever you like in _AppStart.cshtml. For example, consider the following _App-Start.cshtml:

```
@{ AppState["AppStartTime"] = DateTime.Now; }
```

Once this snippet executes, the `AppState["AppStartTime"]` property will contain the timestamp of the very first page hit. `AppState` is a global collection that all views can access, so it makes a good candidate to store global variables.

In order to test it out, create a simple Razor view, *StartTime.cshtml*:

```
The application started at: @AppState["AppStartTime"]
```

The first request to any page on the site triggers the *_AppStart.cshtml* code to execute, setting the value of the `AppState["AppStartTime"]` property once. To verify this, hit the *StartTime.cshtml* page multiple times, refreshing the page and visiting other pages in the site, and then coming back to *StartTime.cshtml*:

```
Application Start Time: 6/17/2011 1:48:27 AM
```

Regardless of how many other pages you visit or how many times you visit them, the value of `@AppState["AppStartTime"]` will remain the same for the entire time the application process continues to live.

 Keep in mind that, though code in the *_AppStart.cshtml* template only gets executed once per application, applications can restart often. When this happens, the application needs to be initialized again and the *_AppStart.cshtml* code executes once more. In most scenarios, this is the behavior you want and expect; however, keep in mind that this code might get executed multiple times a day, depending on how often your application stops and starts.

Executing Code Every Time a Page Executes

Though it might be useful to execute code when the web application starts up, what about scenarios in which code should be executed not just once, but every time someone browses to a page? Luckily, Razor has another special file named *_PageStart.cshtml*, which executes before every single page request. Because of this, *_PageStart.cshtml* makes an excellent location for common code and logic that would otherwise be duplicated in many pages.

One of the best examples of duplicated code is something you've already seen several times in this chapter: the layout page. Here's an example to refresh your memory:

```
@{ Layout = "~/_Layout.cshtml"; }
<div>Some markup here</div>
```

Layouts allow multiple pages to rely on a single layout page to maintain a consistent look and feel across pages. Thus, in order for multiple pages to specify the same layout page, those pages all have to write the same code (namely, `@{ Layout = "~/_Lay out.cshtml"; }` in this example). This makes layout assignments excellent candidates for the *_PageStart.cshtml* file. To execute the layout line for every page within a folder, create a new file named *_PageStart.cshtml* in that folder containing the following:

```
@{ Layout = "~/_Layout.cshtml"; }
```

With this new *_PageStart.cshtml* file in place, the layout assignment line in each individual file can be removed and every page will use the same layout.

Wrapping Views with _PageStart.cshtml Logic

Most of the time you will use *_PageStart.cshtml* templates to run code before pages execute, but *_PageStart.cshtml* templates actually let you execute code and markup both before *and* after the page content. In fact, it's quite easy! Like the RenderBody() method available to layout pages, *_PageStart.cshtml* templates define the @RunPage() method, which controls where in the template the requested page content will execute.

To illustrate, let's say that you are worried that some pages in a folder may cause an error, but instead of showing the user the error, you'd like to show a custom message instead. One of the ways to handle this scenario is to create a *_PageStart.cshtml* template that wraps the page execution in a **try/catch** block and show the custom message:

```
@{
    try {
        RunPage();
    }
    catch {
        <div class="error">
            We're sorry, but we could not process your order at this time.
        </div>
    }
}
```

This template will catch any exceptions that occur during page processing and render a friendly error message instead:

```
<div class="error">
    We're sorry, but we could not process your order at this time.
</div>
```

Executing Multiple _PageStart.cshtml Templates

_PageStart.cshtml templates affect not only Razor views in the same folder, but in all descendant folders as well. In addition, defining another *_PageStart.cshtml* template deeper in the folder structure does not replace the parent template. Every *_PageStart.cshtml* template discovered in a view's folder hierarchy will execute. *_PageStart.cshtml* templates execute in the order they're discovered, starting from the root of the website down to the view's folder.

Let's create multiple levels of *_PageStart.cshtml* templates to see what happens. We'll use the following folder structure:

```
/
    _Layout.cshtml
    _PageStart.cshtml
    Default.cshtml
    /Level1
```

```
    _Layout.cshtml
    _PageStart.cshtml
    Default.cshtml
    /Level2
        _Layout.cshtml
        _PageStart.cshtml
        Default.cshtml
```

The files contain the following:

/_PageStart.cshtml

```
@{
    Layout = "~/_Layout.cshtml";
    Context.Trace.Write("Root _PageStart.cshtml");
}
<div>Root Folder</div>
```

/Level1/_PageStart.cshtml

```
@{
    Layout = "~/Level1/_Layout.cshtml";
    Context.Trace.Write("Level 1 _PageStart.cshtml");
}
<div>Level 1</div>
```

/Level1/Default.cshtml

```
<div>Layout: @Layout</div>
<div>Level 1 Default.cshtml page content</div>
```

/Level2/_PageStart.cshtml

```
@{
    Layout = "~/Level2/_Layout.cshtml";
    Context.Trace.Write("Level 2 _PageStart.cshtml");
}
<div>Level 2</div>
```

/Level2/Default.cshtml

```
<div>Layout: @Layout</div>
<div>Level 2 Default.cshtml page content</div>
```

The *_PageStart.cshtml* at each level overrides the current layout, setting it to the that level's *_Layout.cshtml*. To show that *_PageStart.cshtml* can contain both code and content, each one includes a line of content in addition to the layout code. During page rendering, each page's respective *_PageStart.cshtml* templates will render, starting from the root folder level and ending with the view's folder.

Thus, a call to */Level1/Default.cshtml* will render the following:

```
<div>Root</div>
<div>Level 1</div>
<div>Layout: ~/Level1/_Layout.cshtml</div>
<div>Level 1 Default.cshtml page content</div>
```

Likewise, a call to */Level2/Default.cshtml* will render the following:

```
<div>Root</div>
<div>Level 1</div>
<div>Level 2</div>
<div>Layout: ~/Level2/_Layout.cshtml</div>
<div>Level 2 Default.cshtml page content</div>
```

You may have noticed that the *_PageStart.cshtml* templates contain calls to `Con text.Trace.Write`, writing to the ASP.NET `Trace` object. The ASP.NET `Trace` object is a effective option for lightweight logging. Adding ASP.NET's tracing capabilities for logging page requests is another great use for the *_PageStart.cshtml* template. Placing the logging logic in a centralized location like the *_PageStart.cshtml* template not only reduces duplication of logging code, it also ensures that every page request gets logged.

 Though being able to add code in one place and have it execute in many pages is a powerful feature, it can also be incredibly dangerous. Always keep in mind that the code you chose to execute in your *PageStart.cshtml* templates will execute with *every* request. When *_PageStart.cshtml* templates contain code that consumes a lot of resources or takes a long time to execute, it can quickly destroy the performance of your site.

CHAPTER 4

Razor and ASP.NET MVC

First introduced in early 2008, ASP.NET MVC provided an alternative approach to developing web applications on the ASP.NET platform. As the name indicates, ASP.NET MVC embraces the Model-View-Controller (MVC) architecture, an approach favoring the separation of concerns between application layers. ASP.NET MVC views are much more HTML-focused than views in other frameworks such as Web Forms. Razor complements ASP.NET MVC quite nicely because its simplistic and elegant syntax produces a seamless transition between markup and code, allowing the markup to remain the main focus and not fade into a sea of code-specific syntax.

This chapter will provide a brief introduction to the ASP.NET MVC framework as well as demonstrate how to leverage the Razor syntax to create clean and effective ASP.NET MVC views.

Installing ASP.NET MVC

To begin developing ASP.NET MVC websites using Razor, you'll need to have at least ASP.NET MVC version 3. The Web Platform Installer is the easiest way to install ASP.NET MVC 3.

To begin installation using the Web Platform Installer, visit the ASP.NET MVC website (*http://asp.net/mvc*) and find the big button that says "Install Visual Studio Express" (or something similar).

Regardless of what you have installed on your system prior to running the Web Platform installer, clicking Install will download and install everything you need to start developing ASP.NET MVC 3 applications using Razor.

The Model-View-Controller Architecture

The MVC architecture comprises three layers, each with unique and independent responsibilities:

Model
> Represents the core business/domain data and logic, typically with POCOs (Plain Old CLR Objects), devoid of technology-specific implementations

View
> Responsible for transforming a Model or Models into a response sent to the user (typically HTML)

Controller
> Interprets incoming web requests, managing the interaction between the user and the model (typically through database queries, web services calls, etc.) and building a Model for the View to consume

In the course of an ASP.NET MVC website request, the platform locates and executes the corresponding controller method, also called the *action*. The result of this action is almost always an `ActionResult`. The most widely used type is the `ViewResult`—an `ActionResult` indicating which view the framework should respond to the request with. Following ASP.NET MVC's strict separation of concerns, it is not the controller that is responsible for rendering HTML. Instead, the ASP.NET MVC framework passes the `ActionResult` from the controller to the View Engine, which handles the conversion of a `ViewResult` into rendered HTML to send back to the client.

ASP.NET MVC View Engines

The initial ASP.NET MVC releases shipped with the Web Forms View Engine, which allowed developers to create views with the popular and mature Web Forms syntax. Ironically, the very aspect that makes the Web Forms View Engine such a great fit for new ASP.NET MVC developers—its popularity—is also its biggest drawback. Despite the fact that they are based on the same underlying platform (the ASP.NET framework), the ASP.NET MVC and Web Forms approaches and architectures are fundamentally different in many ways. Thus, while the Web Forms syntax may be second nature to developers creating applications on the Web Forms platform, those same developers may be tempted to try to leverage the Web Forms platform in MVC views...with disastrous results.

The Razor View Engine

The early 2011 ASP.NET MVC 3 release added the Razor View Engine as part of the framework, offering an alternative to the Web Forms View Engine. The Razor View Engine provides developers with a full stack of APIs that leverage the powerful and lightweight Razor syntax, allowing developers to write simpler views that more effectively and efficiently target the MVC architecture.

The Razor View Engine works in much the same way as the Web Forms View Engine, in that views are stored in physical files in the same conventions-based folder structure. Developers author these files using the Razor syntax to create a hybrid document of code and markup. Then at runtime—also as with the Web Forms View Engine—the ASP.NET MVC framework compiles the Razor templates into .NET classes and executes the compiled classes to render responses for requests to the site. The following sections explain each of these steps in detail.

Differentiating Razor syntax and API implementations

It is important to note that the Razor syntax, the Razor API, and implementations built on top of the Razor API are three different things. Previous chapters showcased Web-Matrix examples of the Razor syntax as well as WebMatrix implementations built on top of the Razor API. Likewise, the Razor View Engine also leverages the Razor syntax and API, but also adds subtle enhancements to better suit ASP.NET MVC views.

Though many of the examples shown in previous chapters are relevant to Razor views in ASP.NET MVC, ASP.NET MVC implements quite a few features either differently or not at all. As you read on, keep this in mind, and look for the portions of the book that point out and explain these differences.

Implementing a Blog Site Using ASP.NET MVC

To illustrate how to write Razor views in an ASP.NET MVC application, let's revisit the WebMatrix blog website and rewrite it "the MVC way." To start out, open up Visual Studio and choose File → New Project..., and then select the ASP.NET MVC 3 Web Application option. Name the new project MvcRazorBlog, as shown in Figure 4-1.

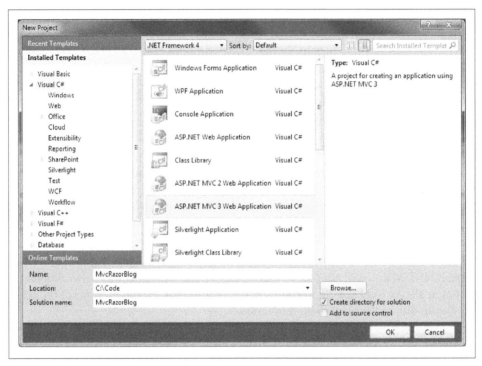

Figure 4-1. Creating a new MVC application

Then, from the New ASP.NET MVC 3 Project Wizard, select the Empty site template and the Razor View Engine (these should be the default settings); Figure 4-2 provides an example.

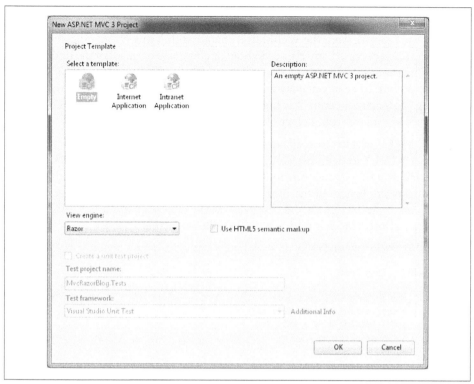

Figure 4-2. The ASP.NET MVC 3 Project Wizard

Once completed, your project should resemble the directory structure shown in Figure 4-3.

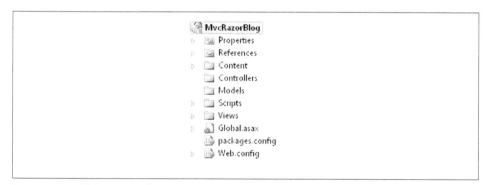

Figure 4-3. Folder structure for a new ASP.NET MVC project

The Model

The blog site example from the WebMatrix chapter didn't involve an official "model." That is, you never created any classes to hold and manage data; all of the data interaction used method calls directly to the database and saved the results in local dynamic variables. WebMatrix can get away with accessing and using the data directly because of the page-based architecture it is built on; every page is responsible for its own data access (with assistance from helper objects) and for manipulating that data.

ASP.NET MVC's architecture dictates that the Model and the View are two separate entities, so in order to demonstrate the Razor syntax within ASP.NET MVC's Razor View Engine, you should create a model that can hold and manage the site's data. Since you've already implemented the blog site once, you already know what data the site uses. To create the Model for the ASP.NET MVC blog site, add a new class named Post to the website's Models folder, with the following code:

```
namespace MvcRazorBlog.Models
{
    public class Post
    {
        public long ID { get; set; }
        public string Title { get; set; }
        public string Body { get; set; }
    }
}
```

Since the blog site doesn't require very complex data, the Post class is all that's needed at this point. Once it's in place, you can create the Controller that will populate the Post class with data from the database and pass it to the View.

The Controller

The default Empty site template chosen earlier expects a controller named HomeCon troller, which ASP.NET MVC adds to the Controllers folder by convention. To create an empty controller, right-click on the Controllers folder and select Add → Controller..., entering the name HomeController.

The wizard will ask you if you'd like it to generate Create, Update, Delete, and Details actions for you. We won't use those actions in this book, but feel free to let the wizard generate them for you if you're interested to see what they look like. The wizard will create a new class file with one action named Index:

```
using System.Web.Mvc;

namespace MvcRazorBlog.Controllers
{
    public class HomeController : Controller
    {
        public ActionResult Index()
        {
```

```
            return View();
        }
    }
}
```

According to ASP.NET MVC's default routes, the HomeController's Index action handles requests for the site's home page (the root of the site without specifying any file or folder names). The behavior we want to implement in the Index action directly correlates to logic used in the sample WebMatrix site's *Default.cshtml* page in Chapter 2. So, the next step is to reproduce the same data access logic that the *Default.cshtml* page uses to retrieve Post data.

Data access with Entity Framework code first

For better or worse, ASP.NET MVC does not offer the same Database object included in the WebMatrix platform. Instead, Microsoft's Entity Framework 4.1 (and up) and its Code First functionality make data access just as easy as it is in WebMatrix, or perhaps more so.

To get started with Entity Framework Code First, you'll need to install it using the NuGet Package Manager, a Visual Studio extension installed as part of the ASP.NET MVC 3 install process.

Using the NuGet Package Manager

The Package Manager has two modes:

The graphical user interface
> The NuGet Package Manager has a graphical user interface that makes it easy to search for, install, update, and uninstall packages for a project. You can access the graphical Package Manager interface by right-clicking the website project in the Solution Explorer and selecting the Add Library Package Reference... option.

Console Mode
> The Library Package Manager Console Mode is a Visual Studio window containing an integrated PowerShell prompt specially configured for Library Package Manager access. If you do not see the Package Manager Console window already open in Visual Studio, you can access the window via the Tools → Library Package Manager → Package Manager Console menu.

To install a package from the Package Manager Console window, simply type the command **Install-Package _Package Name_**. In the case of the Entity Framework package, execute the command **Install-Package EntityFramework**. The Package Manager Console should show its progress as it downloads and installs the package into your project. After you complete the **Install-Package** step, you should see your assembly referenced in your project's References list.

After it's installed, the only other step you need to take in order to use the Entity Framework Code First framework is to create a custom class that derives from the

`System.Data.Entity.DbContext` class, which tells Entity Framework which objects you'd like to persist and retrieve from the database. A working `DbContext` implementation can be as simple as the following:

```
using System.Data.Entity;
using MvcRazorBlog.Models;

public class BlogContext : DbContext
{
    public DbSet<Post> Posts;
}
```

This code extends the `DbContext` class, exposing a single property (`Posts`) of type `DBSet<Post>`. It is the `DbSet<Post>` portion of this property that indicates to Entity Framework that you'd like to use the `Post` class as your model for data access and that these objects can be found in the Posts table (corresponding to the name of the property) in the database.

That's all that's needed in regards to setup and configuration; Entity Framework relies on "convention over configuration" to determine the rest. Entity Framework will even create the database for you if it does not exist when you attempt to access it!

Querying an Entity Framework Code First data context is even easier than writing one. All you need to do is create an instance of a `DbContext` and start making standard LINQ calls against the `DbSet<TModel>` properties defined on the context.

Thus, retrieving all of the Posts from the Blog database from the `HomeController`'s `Index` action is trivial:

```
public class HomeController {
    public ActionResult Index()
    {
        var posts = new BlogContext().Posts;
        return View("Index");
    }
}
```

Once the `Index` action retrieves the blog post data from the database, it needs to select the appropriate View and pass the post data to that View. Since the MVC pattern deliberately decouples views and controllers, the controller cannot directly communicate with the selected view to provide the view with the data it needs. In order to get around this limitation, ASP.NET MVC relies on an intermediary dictionary via a property named `ViewData`. Controllers and views both contain this property, so it is easily accessible in both layers. Here is the updated `Index` action, adding a line of code to assign the blog post data to the `ViewData` dictionary for use in the views that you will create in the coming sections:

```
public class HomeController {
    public ActionResult Index()
    {
        var posts = new BlogContext().Posts;
```

```
        ViewData["Posts"] = posts;

        return View("Index");
    }
}
```

Though passing values to views through the ViewData dictionary works just fine, "magic values" (string constants referenced in multiple places) like "Posts" can become difficult to manage and maintain. Additionally, the ViewData dictionary is not strongly-typed, so Visual Studio cannot provide you with IntelliSense on any values passed into it. Instead of the ViewData dictionary, the preferred approach for passing data from controllers to views is through the model parameter of the View() helper method.

Below you can see the Index action updated to pass the Posts data via the View() helper method:

Index action retrieving blog posts and passing them to the view

```
public ActionResult Index()
{
    var posts = new BlogContext().Posts;
    return View("Index", posts);
}
```

At this point—even though you have not yet created the View required to render HTML to the user—you should be able to verify that this code works by placing a debug breakpoint on the final return View("Index"); line and hitting F5 to run the website. If everything works, execution should stop at the breakpoint and the posts variable should contain a list of Post objects with the data from your database!

Convention versus Configuration

To make website development easier and help developers be more productive, ASP.NET MVC relies on the concept of "convention over configuration" whenever possible. What this means is that, instead of relying on explicit configuration settings, ASP.NET MVC simply assumes that developers will follow certain conventions as they create website components.

The previous section applied several conventions when creating the HomeController and its Index action. The first convention was placing the controller in the project's Controllers folder. Though not required for the application to compile and function, keeping your controllers in the Controllers folder is a standard practice. The second convention was the name of the controller, HomeController. Since it is a very good practice to give classes descriptive names, standard conventions recommend applying the "Controller" suffix to controller class names. When referring to the controller throughout the application, however, it is much more straightforward to simply refer to "Home" instead of the full name, "HomeController."

The ASP.NET MVC framework addresses this conflict during the application's startup phase, when it searches through all of the website's assemblies, registering classes that extend ASP.NET MVC's `ControllerBase` base class (using the base class as yet another convention). As the framework locates classes that derive from `ControllerBase`, it adds them to its internal dictionary using the class's name—after removing the "Controller" suffix—as the dictionary key. Thus, even though the controller is named "HomeController," the rest of the application can simply refer to it as "Home."

At first glance, the concept of convention over configuration may seem trivial. However, when taken altogether over the course of a large site, many of these seemingly small or meaningless optimizations can really add up to significant time savings, improved code readability, and increased developer productivity.

Authoring ASP.NET MVC Views with the Razor Syntax

Since WebMatrix and ASP.NET MVC Razor views share the Razor syntax to create views, the easiest way to create a view in the demo ASP.NET MVC blog site is to copy the markup we already created in the WebMatrix example. First, however, you need to create a new view to contain the copied markup.

Adding Razor Views to an ASP.NET MVC Application

The ASP.NET MVC platform adds several convenient and helpful extensions to the Visual Studio IDE. One of the extensions adds two new context menu items, named Add View and Go to View, that show up when you right-click on a controller action. These menu items make it very easy to create and navigate to the views associated with an action.

The Add View context menu item is the quickest and easiest way to create a new view. To create a new view for the `Index` action in the HomeController of the demo blog application, simply right-click anywhere within the `Index` action, and then choose Add View. This should pop up the Add View Wizard.

The Add View Wizard prepopulates several of the fields by using conventions. In this case, the value in the prepopulated "View name" field is "Index," the name of the controller action from which we clicked on the Add View context menu. The "View engine" field lets developers choose which syntax to use for creating views. The default view engine is "Razor (CSHTML)," which means the Razor C# syntax (as opposed to, say, the Razor Visual Basic .NET syntax).

Ignore the rest of the fields in the wizard; later sections of the book will revisit them in detail. For now, just click the Add button and let's write a view!

Clicking the Add button tells Visual Studio to create a new view file for you at the appropriate location within the project. Figure 4-4 shows the contents of the project's Views folder after the Add View dialog executes.

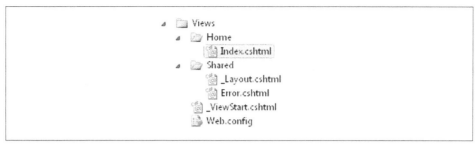

Figure 4-4. Views folder structure

As you can see, the Views folder contains child folders named Home and Shared. Why are these folders named this way? You guessed it: yet another convention! By default, ASP.NET MVC assumes that all website views exist somewhere underneath the Views folder. Further, ASP.NET MVC looks for child folders underneath the root Views folder with folder names corresponding to the names of controllers in the application. Using all of this information—along with the information we provided—the Add View dialog chose to create a file named *Index.cshtml* in a new folder under the root Views folder named Home (corresponding to the `HomeController` controller class the Add View menu action originated from). Leveraging the power of conventions, Visual Studio was able to do all of this with just two clicks!

Why the .cshtml file extension?

In the course of rendering a view, the ASP.NET MVC runtime will use the view's file extension to determine how to compile the markup in the view. For instance, ASP.NET MVC can safely assume that a file with the *.aspx* extension uses the Web Forms syntax, whereas a view with the *.cshtml* extension contains Razor markup. Both ASP.NET MVC Razor views and WebMatrix Web Pages use the *.cshtml* extension for Razor views that leverage the C# language and *.vbhtml* for Razor views that leverage Visual Basic .NET. ASP.NET MVC supports both languages equally—they can even be used together in the same project!

Writing ASP.NET MVC Razor View Markup

After creating the new file, replace the entire contents of this new view with this markup:

```
<h1>My Blog</h1>

@foreach(var post in Model) {
    <div>
        <h3>@post.Title</h3>
        <div>@post.Body</div>
    </div>
}
```

This should look familiar; it's very similar to the markup you used to create the home page in the WebMatrix blog site. The biggest difference is that, instead of pulling the posts data from the database, the markup iterates over the View's `Model` property, which represents the model data passed to the View from the Controller in "Data access with Entity Framework code first" on page 57.

At this point, you have everything in place to generate a web page: the Controller is retrieving data from the database and passing that data to the View, which the View can then use to render dynamic HTML. To see it in action, hit F5 to execute the website. If you have data in the Posts database, it should render something similar to the following:

```
<h1>My Blog</h1>

<div>
    <h3>Test Post #1</h3>
    <div>This is the first test post</div>
</div>
<div>
    <h3>Test Post #2</h3>
    <div>This is the second test post</div>
</div>
<div>
    <h3>Test Post #3</h3>
    <div>This is the third test post</div>
</div>
```

Strongly-Typed Views

The `Model` property present in the `WebViewPage` base class from which all ASP.NET MVC views derive is dynamically-typed by default. This means that it uses .NET 4.0's dynamic type, delaying the specification of the type until runtime. Thus, Controller Actions and other parts of the ASP.NET MVC framework can populate this field with any type and the views can apply the concept of "duck-typing" to work with a variety of types. As long as the model object contains the properties with the name that the view expects, any type will do!

If this "fast and loose" approach concerns you, you are in good company. You are also in luck: ASP.NET MVC adds the `@model` keyword to Razor's vernacular, which allows views to specify the type of their `Model` property. The `@model` keyword follows the syntax `@model Class Name`.

To show the `@model` keyword in action, let's modify the previous example and turn it into a strongly-typed view by specifying a `@model`:

A strongly-typed view

```
@model IEnumerable<MvcRazorBlog.Models.Post>

@section Header {
    <h1>My Blog</h1>
```

```
    }

    @foreach(var post in Model) {
        @RenderPage("~/Posts/_Post.cshtml", new { post = post })
    }
```

And just like that, the `Model` property is now strongly-typed as an `IEnumerable<MvcRa` `zorBlog.Models.Post>`, ready for use without additional casting.

By default, all ASP.NET MVC Razor views inherit from the `System.Web.Mvc.WebView` `Page` class. However, views that specify a model type using the `@model` keyword inherit from the generic version of `WebViewPage`: `System.Web.Mvc.WebViewPage<TModel>`. With the exception of a few Razor keywords outlined in the first chapter, the bulk of ASP.NET MVC's view-related functionality (such as the `@Html` and `@Url` helpers) exists as properties or extension methods off of the `WebViewPage` class.

What the `@model` keyword actually does is tell ASP.NET MVC to add a generic parameter to the base page type. In other words, an ASP.NET MVC view without the `@model` keyword derives from the `WebViewPage` base class like so:

```
public class Index : WebViewPage {
    /* Class stuff in here */
}
```

But when the `@model` keyword is applied, as in the previous example, Razor adds the specified type as a generic parameter to the generated class. For example:

```
@model IEnumerable<MvcRazorBlog.Models.Post>
```

will generate the view:

```
public class Index : WebViewPage<IEnumerable<MvcRazorBlog.Models.Post>> {
    /* Class stuff in here */
}
```

Changing the Base Class

Despite the great functionality it provides, you will inevitably come across scenarios where the `System.Web.Mvc.WebViewPage` class simply doesn't cut it. In cases where you need more functionality than the `WebViewPage` class offers, Razor provides the `@inher` `its` keyword, which lets you specify any base class you want—even your own custom base class. One of the most common uses of the `@inherits` keyword is to specify a custom base class that extends the `WebViewPage` class, adding custom functionality through properties and methods.

Let's say that you have created a bunch of helper methods and you want some kind of shortcut to access your helper methods from within your views. The quickest way to provide easy access to custom helper methods is to write extension methods around the `@Html` or `@Url`, since they already exist in the `WebViewPage` class. However, if you like to keep your helper methods separate from the core ASP.NET MVC functionality, you can choose to create your own helper object that acts much like `@Html` or `@Url`, and then add an instance of that custom helper object to a custom base class. The `BlogHelper` class below shows an example of such a custom helper object. The custom base class (`BlogViewPage`) exposes the custom helper object via a custom property:

```
public class BlogHelper
{
    private readonly UrlHelper _urlHelper;

    public BlogHelper(UrlHelper urlHelper) {
        _urlHelper = urlHelper;
    }

    public MvcHtmlString BlogPostLink(int postId) {
        var tag = new TagBuilder("a");
        tag.AddCssClass("blog-post");
        tag.Attributes["href"] = _urlHelper.Action("Post", "Posts");

        return new MvcHtmlString(tag.ToString());
    }
}

namespace MvcRazorBlog {
    public abstract class BlogViewPage : BlogViewPage<dynamic>
    {
    }

    public abstract class BlogViewPage<TModel> : WebViewPage<TModel>
    {
        protected BlogHelper Blog
        {
            get { return new BlogHelper(Url); }
        }
    }
}
```

The first thing you'll notice about the custom base class `BlogViewPage` is that there are actually two of them—one that accepts a generic `TModel` parameter, and one that is not generic. The reason you should create both is so that you continue to have the option of strongly-typed views. Without the generic version of this class, you would not be able to use the `@model` keyword to specify the view's Model type. Likewise, if the non-generic `BlogViewPage` doesn't exist, all of the views that depend on the `BlogViewPage` custom base class would be required to specify a `TModel` parameter (i.e., they'd need to be strongly-typed views).

The next thing you'll notice about `BlogViewPage` is how tiny it is. Because the aim is to merely extend the core ASP.NET MVC functionality and not replace it, `BlogViewPage` can derive from ASP.NET MVC's `WebViewPage<TModel>` and in doing so, carry along all of the core functionality. With the core functionality in place, `BlogViewPage`'s only goal is to expose the new custom `Blog` property, a simple property that just returns a new instance of the custom `BlogHelper` helper class.

With the `BlogViewPage` created, referencing it is as simple as adding the `@inherits` keyword to any Razor views that require it:

View inheriting from custom base class

```
@inherits MvcRazorBlog.BlogViewPage

<span>Here's a link to Post #123:</span>
@Blog.BlogPostLink(123)
```

Here you can see that the view inherits from `BlogViewPage`, then refers to the `@Blog.Blog PostLink()` method on the custom `Blog` property.

 ASP.NET MVC does not let you specify both the `@inherits` keyword and the `@model` keyword in the same view.

Since ASP.NET MVC does not let you specify both the `@inherits` keyword and the `@model` keyword in the same view, you need to specify the model type (the `TModel` generic parameter) directly in the `@inherits` statement in order to refer to the strongly-typed version of a custom base class. Thus, to change the previous example from weakly-typed to strongly-typed, you would change its `@inherits` statement like so:

```
@inherits MvcRazorBlog.BlogViewPage<AdminViewModel>
```

The custom base class approach offers greater levels of customization and productivity in your websites. Custom base classes are not only easy to create and reference, but they are also a great way to provide quick and easy access to customized, application-specific functionality across all views in an application. Whenever the default `WebView Page` class just doesn't cut it, consider implementing your own base class!

Applying Custom Base Classes to Multiple Views

When all of your views need to derive from the same custom base class, having to add the `@inherits` keyword to all of them is not only tedious, but it's also difficult to maintain. Luckily, ASP.NET MVC offers an alternative approach to specifying the default base class for all Razor views: the `system.web.webPages.razor > pages > pageBase Type` configuration attribute. To modify this attribute, open the *web.config* file located in your application's Views folder, and then locate the line that looks like this: `<pages pageBaseType="System.Web.Mvc.WebViewPage">`. This is where ASP.NET MVC's default base page type comes from. To use your own base page type, simply replace the reference to `System.Web.Mvc.WebViewPage` with the full type name of your base class type (e.g., `<pages pageBaseType="MvcRazorBlog.BlogViewPage">`). After saving the modified *web.config*, every view in your application should use your custom base page type.

Layouts and Content Pages

You may have noticed that the markup in "Strongly-Typed Views" on page 62 included an `<h1>` header tag and a list of `<div>`s with blog post content, but no surrounding HTML document markup like `<html>` or `<body>` tags. This is because when you created the new view and left the "Use a layout or master page" option checked and the text box empty you told ASP.NET MVC to create a "content page," a page that relies on a Layout to define the structure of the page.

Chapter 3 discusses Razor layouts and content pages in depth and all of those concepts apply to ASP.NET MVC Razor views as well. In addition to that functionality, however, ASP.NET MVC adds an additional layer of abstraction and helper methods to simplify working with Razor views.

The most significant example of ASP.NET MVC Razor view helpers is the `HtmlHelper.Partial()` method, whose syntax is very similar to the Razor `@Render Page()` method, but instead of accepting a static filename, the `HtmlHelper.Partial()` method expects a simple view name, which ASP.NET MVC then uses to locate and render the appropriate view.

For example, "Strongly-Typed Views" on page 62 contains a call to `@RenderPage()`:

```
@RenderPage("Posts/_Post.cshtml", post)
```

In this snippet, *Posts/_Post.cshtml* refers to a physical file in the website. In comparison, this same call as an ASP.NET MVC `HtmlHelper.Partial()` would look like this:

```
@Html.Partial("_Post", post)
```

The `Partial()` method call still refers to the same partial view, except the location and exact filename of that view are now abstracted away. That is, instead of the view dictating the exact file location of *Posts/_Post.cshtml*, ASP.NET MVC expects a request to render the partial view named *_Post*, leaving the implementation details of the *_Post* view up to the framework to figure out. Though in this instance ASP.NET MVC will, in fact, execute the *Posts/_Post.cshtml* view, consider what would happen if a developer decided to move the view to a different folder or even rewrite the view in VB.NET (thus changing the view's extension to *.vbhtml*). That's just fine; as long as ASP.NET MVC is able to match the view name to a file that it knows about, it will render it no matter what its physical location or what language it's written in.

Razor View File Locations

At this point, you may be wondering just how ASP.NET MVC is able to match the name of a view to its physical location in the filesystem. For that matter, how does ASP.NET MVC differentiate between two views that share the same file name, yet reside in different folders? The answer to both of these questions is the same: the Razor View Engine!

When a controller action returns a `ViewResult`, ASP.NET MVC knows that it needs to render a view, so it asks all of its registered view engines if they can figure out how to locate and render the requested view. Between the routing information for the current request and the `ViewResult`, the view engines should have all the information they need: the view name and the name of the controller that handled the request. By convention, all ASP.NET MVC views live in subfolders under the *~/Views* folder.

In one of the previous examples, the `HomeController` requested the view named Index. Let's see how the Razor View Engine tries to locate the Index view.

Controller Views

The first place the Razor View Engine will look for a view is in the folder with the same name as the controller that handled the request. Given the request from the `HomeCon troller` for the Index view, the view engine will check if the C# Razor template *~/Views/Home/Index.cshtml* exists. If not, the engine tries again, this time looking for the VB.NET Razor template named *~/Views/Home/Index.vbhtml*. Though C# and VB.NET are the only languages Razor currently supports, the same process would apply for any new languages that might be added (for example, the engine might look for *~/Views/Home/Index.fshtml* for an F# template if such an implementation existed).

When the view engine locates a file, it stops looking immediately and returns the first file it found. Otherwise, it continues down its list of search paths to look in the Shared folder.

Locating Razor Views

Armed with all the information about the controller that handled the current request, the Razor View Engine relies on the default view locator logic to build a list of possible locations in which the requested view may reside. After compiling this list, the view engine simply iterates over it, returning the first match it finds. As you might expect, the view engine prefers more specific views—views defined in the folder with the same name as the Controller that requested them—over views in the Shared folder, so the more specific views will appear higher on the list than shared views.

This example illustrates this point, showing what the list of possible view locations might look like in order to locate a request for the Index view that generated from a controller named `HomeController`:

The view engine's view candidates

```
~/Views/Home/Index.cshtml
~/Views/Home/Index.vbhtml
~/Views/Shared/Index.cshtml
~/Views/Shared/Index.vbhtml
```

Thus, if the *~/Views/Home/Index.cshtml* view exists, the view engine will choose it and ignore the rest of the list. If, however, *~/Views/Home/Index.cshtml* does not exist, but

~/Views/Shared/Index.cshtml exists instead, the view engine will continue searching down the list, checking each entry, until it discovers that *~/Views/Shared/Index.cshtml* is valid and chooses it.

Shared Views

You may have noticed that the folder list includes references to the Shared folder. The *~/Views/Shared* folder contains views that can be reused by multiple controllers. The Shared folder is created along with the rest of the initial application artifacts by the ASP.NET MVC website template and initially contains the basic layout and error-handling views (*_Layout.cshtml* and *Error.cshtml*, respectively), two perfect examples of reusable views.

Views in ASP.NET MVC Areas

The Areas feature of ASP.NET MVC allows a web application to be split up into multiple sections ("Areas"), enabling developers to work on each section individually in relative isolation. Though an in-depth discussion of ASP.NET MVC Areas would be outside the scope of this book, Areas are effectively a "website within a website" and, as such, it is worth discussing how Areas affect the views that are created within them.

For example, let's add an Area named "Administration" to the demo blog site. To add an Area, right-click on the ASP.NET MVC project and select the Add... context menu option, which should pop up the submenu shown in Figure 4-5 and specify the Area name "Administration" when prompted.

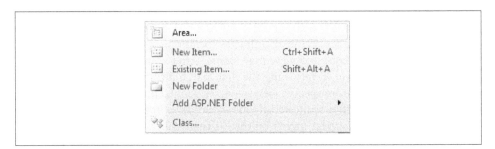

Figure 4-5. Add Area context menu option

As Figure 4-6 shows, ASP.NET MVC Areas define a folder structure within the main website that follows the same standard Controllers, Models, and Views convention. The primary difference is that the root folder of this structure is not the root folder of the ASP.NET MVC application.

Since Areas use the same folder structure convention, the only significant change they introduce in regard to Views is adding their folders to the list of search folders that the View Engine uses to locate the correct view. For example, a ViewResult from an action

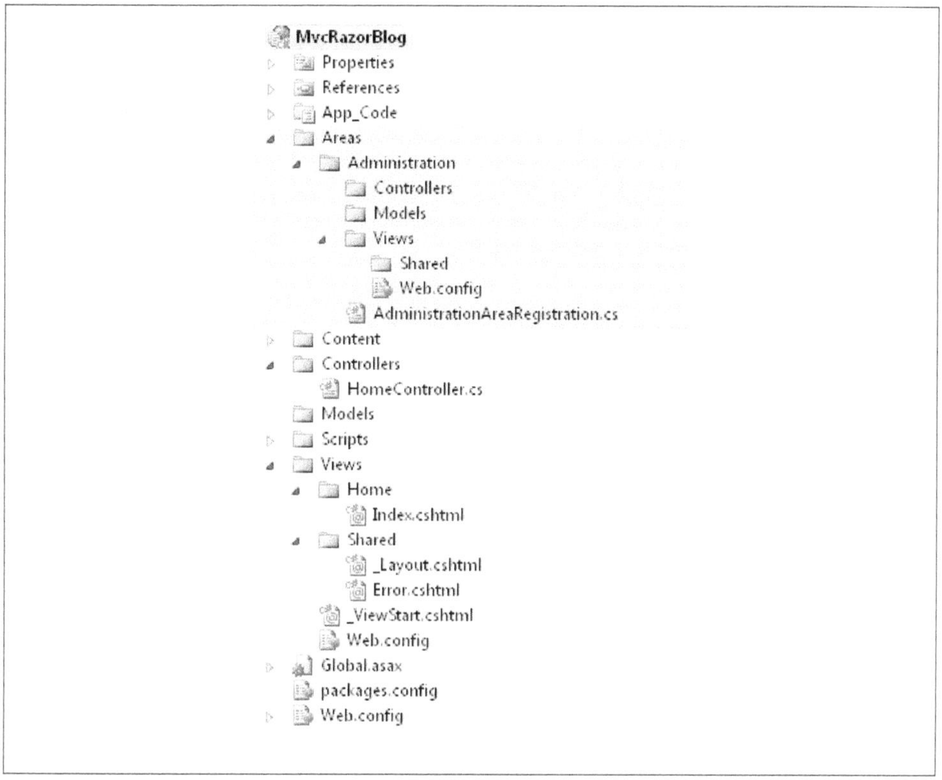

Figure 4-6. Website folder structure with an Area

within the Administration Area's `DashboardController` would modify a default search folder list:

```
~/Views/Dashboard/Index.cshtml
~/Views/Dashboard/Index.vbhtml
~/Views/Shared/Index.cshtml
~/Views/Shared/Index.vbhtml
```

to include the Views folder within the Admin area:

```
~/Areas/Administration/Views/Dashboard/Index.cshtml
~/Areas/Administration/Views/Dashboard/Index.vbhtml
~/Areas/Administration/Views/Shared/Index.cshtml
~/Areas/Administration/Views/Shared/Index.vbhtml
~/Views/Dashboard/Index.cshtml
~/Views/Dashboard/Index.vbhtml
~/Views/Shared/Index.cshtml
~/Views/Shared/Index.vbhtml
```

Outside of the modified search path, developing views within Areas is the same as developing views located in the main website.

The way the Razor View Engine and the Web Forms View Engine look for views is almost exactly the same. Both engines look in the folder with the name of the current controller as well as the Shared folder. Both engines also respect the Areas folder as well. In fact, the primary difference in the way the two view engines locate views is the file extension they're looking for: the Razor View Engine searches for *.cshtml* and *.vbhtml* files while the Web Forms View Engine searches for files with the *.aspx* and *.ascx* extensions.

Html and Url Helper Classes

While previous chapters discussed almost everything you need to know to write effective ASP.NET MVC Views, ASP.NET MVC offers a number of additions to the core Razor syntax and API. The most helpful additions are the `HtmlHelper` and `UrlHelper` classes, exposed in ASP.NET MVC Views as the `Html` and `Url` properties, respectively. These two helper methods provide much-needed access to ASP.NET MVC's more advanced and decoupled ways of interacting with Models and other Views.

For example, rather than manually building anchor tags and URLs, ASP.NET MVC offers the `HtmlHelper.ActionLink()` method which accepts a number of varying parameters and emits a complete anchor tag (`<a>`) to the page. The snippet below shows the `HtmlHelper.ActionLink()` method in action:

```
@Html.ActionLink("Site Members", "Members", "Admin")
```

This particular overload of the `HtmlHelper.ActionLink()` method contains three parameters:

1. The link text to show as the inner HTML within the anchor tag
2. The name of the Action referred to (in this case, the `"Members"` action)
3. The name of the Controller containing the Action in parameter #2 (in this case, the `"AdminController"` class)

When executed during view rendering, the snippet produces the following HTML:

```
<a href="/Admin/Members">Site Members</a>
```

While ASP.NET MVC gives developers endless control over the HTML that is rendered to the client, helper methods like these provide a more declarative—and therefore, more maintainable—way to implement site functionality.

The `HtmlHelper.ActionLink()` example is just one of many useful helper methods available on the `Html` and `Url` View properties. Though we will not review all of them at this point, future examples (in fact, almost any ASP.NET MVC example you will see) will leverage these properties quite heavily, so keep an eye out!

ASP.NET MVC's Razor View Page Rendering Life Cycle

ASP.NET leverages a "just in time" (JIT) compilation model in which views are written and deployed as regular text files and only converted into code for ASP.NET to consume at the last possible moment. The "last possible moment" is generally the first request for a view by a visitor to the site. Despite having an entirely different architecture than Web Forms, Razor views share the same deployment and compilation life cycle. The only difference between the two rendering engines is how they turn a text file into an executable class for the web application to use in rendering responses.

Precompiling Razor Views

While the JIT compilation feature of ASP.NET makes it trivial to modify views in a deployed site (with even a simple text editor), this means that the ASP.NET framework must compile them in real time on the web server. This approach has several drawbacks:

Increased wait times
> The first visitors to each page must wait while the view is compiled and rendered. Though compilation typically takes just a few seconds, this delay can be unacceptable for businesses that demand total rendering times of 2 seconds or less.

Increased server resources
> Even the compilation of simple views requires server resources. While compiling a few pages on a simple site may take a small amount of CPU time and memory usage, consider a much larger website with hundreds or thousands of views with hundreds or thousands of users all waiting for their pages to finish compiling!

Delayed discovery of errors
> Since text-based views are only compiled during their first request, they are essentially source code files until that time. Because of this, compilation errors are not exposed until the "last possible moment," which effectively means that compilation errors in views will not be discovered until the website is live on the server.

Luckily, ASP.NET provides you with the ability to precompile views before they are deployed to a web server. That is, you can execute the JIT compilation—the same application that ASP.NET itself uses to compile views—on demand without having to wait for website requests. The application (named `aspnet_compiler.exe`) is located along with the rest of the core .NET Framework libraries and applications (typically *%WINDIR%\Microsoft.NET\Framework\[framework version]*). Thus, if you have the full .NET Framework installed, you have the ability to compile the views in your website, even in your local development environment.

Executing the *aspnet_compiler.exe* application is very straightforward. Assuming the root folder of your website project is *C:\Projects\Website*, execute the following line using the Visual Studio Command Prompt:

```
aspnet_compiler -v / -p "C:\Projects\Website"
```

The compiler will run for a short time (anywhere from a few seconds to a minute or more, depending on the size of your site), and emits warning and error messages as it compiles each view it finds. If you are lucky, the compiler will exit with no messages beyond the "splash screen," indicating that all your views have successfully compiled with no warnings or errors.

Now, let's introduce a compilation error and run the compiler again, which spits out the following error:

```
Test.cshtml(5): error CS0103: The name 'index' does not exist in the current context
```

This line says that the compiler found one error on line 5 of the file *Test.cshtml*: the Razor markup is trying to refer to a variable named `index`, but it is not defined in the page. When the compiler finds warnings or errors such as these, simply edit the respective view to fix the errors and rerun the compiler until the errors go away. Just like the .NET compilers, *aspnet_compiler.exe* does not alter anything in the site, so it can run repeatedly with no side effects.

Using the *aspnet_compiler.exe* tool, you can precompile every view in any ASP.NET website (including Web Forms pages as well) before they are accessible to users, ensuring that the code in your views properly compiles and eliminating unnecessary server resource utilization and visitor wait times.

Precompiling Razor Views in an ASP.NET MVC application

While the command line approach can be very effective, the ASP.NET MVC Web Application project type adds a more integrated option. The project file includes a property named `MvcBuildViews`, which, when enabled, executes the *aspnet_compiler.exe* as part of the build. This setting is disabled by default because of the additional time incurred by running the compiler and needs to be enabled to take effect. The setting is also not accessible via the Visual Studio user interfaces. Despite these drawbacks, enabling view compilation as part of the ASP.NET MVC website build process is quite simple:

1. Open the website's project file with any normal text editor other than Visual Studio (Windows Notepad is just fine)
2. Locate the XML element named `<MvcBuildViews>`, whose value should be `"false"`
3. Modify the value of the `<MvcBuildViews>` element to `"true"`
4. Save and close the updated project file
5. Reload the project in Visual Studio

Once the setting is enabled, all builds will include a new step which executes the *aspnet_compiler.exe*. As Figure 4-7 shows, any warnings or errors show up in Visual Studio's error console, just as any other compile-time errors or warnings.

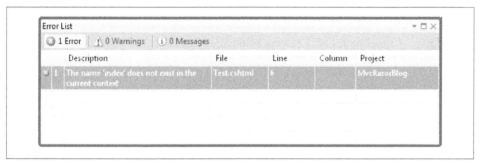

Figure 4-7. MVC view errors in Visual Studio's error list

Compiling views from MSBuild

If you would like to avoid editing the website project file manually and don't like the idea of adding time to every build of your website, there is a middle ground between having the `MvcBuildViews` setting permanently enabled or never enabled. Another application shipped with the .NET Framework, *MSBuild.exe*, provides the ability to execute the same compilation pipeline that Visual Studio itself uses without opening Visual Studio. What's more, *MSBuild.exe* also allows project property settings (like the `MvcBuildViews` setting) to be overridden.

> When you leave the `MvcBuildViews` property disabled in the project file and enable it as an MSBuild flag, you get the best of both worlds: quick compilation times while developing in Visual studio without losing the ability to discover errors in your views. Just remember: it is now up to you to run MSBuild often!

To execute *MSBuild.exe*, open up the Visual Studio Command Prompt (just as you did earlier for *aspnet_compiler.exe*), and then switch to your solution's directory. Then, execute the following line (replacing **SolutionName** with the name of your solution):

```
msbuild /p:MvcBuildViews=true SolutionName
```

The command for the example blog project would be:

```
msbuild /p:MvcBuildViews=true MvcRazorBlog.sln
```

The MSBuild output includes all of the details of the build. Most importantly, the `MvcBuildViews` step executes the *aspnet_compiler.exe* you manually ran before. In addition to eliminating the need to execute *aspnet_compiler.exe* manually, executing *aspnet_compiler.exe* as part of the build script makes the compilation a first-class citizen in the build process. Now, any time a view contains an error, that error will get the visibility it deserves, just like any other error in the site.

Since continuous integration servers like Team Foundation Server or CruiseControl.NET execute MSBuild directly to compile projects, it is very easy to add the MvcBuildViews property to the list of options during your continuous integration builds. If you are using continuous integration to build your ASP.NET MVC websites, I highly recommend you enable this flag during your builds.

CHAPTER 5

The Razor API

Most of this book is dedicated to the Razor syntax and how to use it to interact with the ASP.NET, WebMatrix, and ASP.NET APIs. However, Razor is more than just a syntax; it is backed by a full-fledged API that interprets Razor templates and turns them into executable code (.NET classes) that frameworks such as WebMatrix and ASP.NET MVC can execute to render text.

"How Razor Parses Markup and Code" on page 6 provides a brief glimpse at how the Razor parsing logic works, but there is much more that has to happen to turn a document that uses the Razor syntax ("a Razor template") into rendered HTML. Parsing a Razor template is merely the first step in the process.

Razor Templates: From Markup to .NET Code

Razor templates have a life cycle all their own. Figure 5-1 shows a high-level overview of how Razor templates are used in the course of an application.

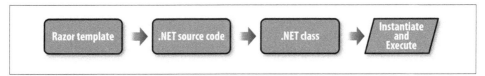

Figure 5-1. The Razor template life cycle

The process of turning Razor markup into .NET code consists of several steps. To illustrate, let's look at how the Razor parser breaks down the following Razor template:

```
<div>
  @foreach(var post in Posts) {
    <div>@post.Title</div>
  }
</div>
```

1. Parse the Razor Template

To begin, the Razor parser analyzes the text (as described in "How Razor Parses Markup and Code" on page 6), breaking it up into "blocks." Each of these blocks represents a section of the template—either markup or code—and they are hierarchical in nature. A good way to think about them is like an XML document, except in addition to text elements, the document also includes code expressions. The Razor parser will generate a markup document with this structure:

```
<Document>
    <Markup><div>\r\n\t</Markup>
    <Statement>
        <Transition>@</Transition>
        <Code>foreach(var post in posts) { </Code>
        <Markup>
            <Markup><div></Markup>
            <Expression>
                <Transition>@</Transition>
                <ImplicitExpression>post.Title</ImplicitExpression>
            </Expression>
            <Markup></div></Markup>
        </Markup>
        <Code> } </Code>
        <Markup></div></Markup>
    </Statement>
    <Markup>\r\n</div></Markup>
</Document>
```

2. Generate .NET Code

After the template is parsed into a tree of nodes, the next step is to translate those nodes into .NET code. The parsed markup from the previous step does not contain enough to build a class by itself; it is missing some very important and fundamental information, such as the class name and namespace. To overcome this obstacle, the Razor API takes a guess at what these values should be, falling back on default values when it cannot make an accurate guess.

With all the information it needs, the Razor class generator generates a relatively simple class. Given the example parsed document from the previous step, the Razor C# code generator will produce the code below. Clearly, this code will not compile as-is; it breaks basic C# language rules, such as using the **override** keyword when there is no base method to override and calling the undefined **Write()** and **WriteLiteral()** methods.

Nobody said that Razor had to generate *working* code, however—making sure the generated class properly compiles and executes is not Razor's responsibility! The Razor code generator is only responsible for translating the parser results into .NET code. This is where frameworks like WebMatrix and ASP.NET MVC come into play, implementing a base class that the generated class can derive from which satisfies the code that Razor generates (i.e., implements the `Write(object)` and `WriteLiteral(object)` methods). Remember, Razor is not a web development framework; it is just an API that makes your web development framework of choice easier to use!

C# code generated by the Razor class generator

```
namespace Razor {
    public class __CompiledTemplate {
        public __CompiledTemplate() {
        }

        public override void Execute() {
            WriteLiteral("<div>\r\n\t");

            @foreach(var post in posts) {
                WriteLiteral("<div>");
                Write(post.Title);
                WriteLiteral("</div>");
            }

            WriteLiteral("\r\n</div>");
        }
    }
}
```

3. Compile Generated Code into an Executable Class

In most cases, the Razor code generator does not produce files that contain code—at least not the kind of text-based code that you or I sit down and write. What the generator produces is a `System.CodeDom.CodeCompileUnit` that contains a collection of metadata that together forms the definition of a class. As its namespace implies, `System.CodeDom.CodeCompileUnit` is part of the .NET Framework, not part of the Razor API, so technically speaking, the Razor API's job is done after it produces the `CodeCompileUnit`.

After the API produces the `CodeCompileUnit`, it is up to the consumer of the Razor API (e.g., ASP.NET MVC or WebMatrix) to compile the `CodeCompileUnit` into an executable class. "Compiling Razor Templates" on page 80 walks you through exactly how this is done.

4. Instantiate and Execute the Generated Class

By this point the Razor API has completed its work and produced an executable class, so technically this step has nothing to do with the Razor API directly. It is, however, the most important step, because this is when the consumer of the generated class (e.g., WebMatrix or ASP.NET MVC) gets to execute the class and reap the benefits of the Razor API's hard work!

As you can see, Razor templates mean nothing by themselves; their only function is to tell the Razor API how to populate the classes it generates, and after that they are never referred to again. In this way, Razor template files actually resemble a designer that lets you use a condensed syntax to produce a .NET class, much like a Visual Studio Settings file.

Meet the Players

Now that you know how a Razor template gets turned into an executable class, it's time to take a tour of the Razor API classes that make it all possible. The basic list is surprisingly short:

System.Web.Razor.Parser.RazorParser
> RazorParser executes the logic discussed in "How Razor Parses Markup and Code" on page 6, mapping a Razor template into an in-memory document that the RazorCodeGenerator can consume. Despite its name, RazorParser does not know anything about HTML or code languages such as C#. Instead, RazorParser relies on other code and markup implementations to perform the actual parsing. For example, the MarkupParser class knows how to interpret HTML markup, and the CSharpCodeParser and VBCodeParser classes know how to parse C# and VB.NET code, respectively. RazorParser merely acts as the coordinator between various markup and code parsing implementations.

System.Web.Razor.Generator.RazorCodeGenerator
> The RazorCodeGenerator class contains the logic for generating .NET code from RazorParser's output. Like RazorParser, the RazorCodeGenerator class itself does not have any knowledge of any specific languages, only general knowledge of how to interpret RazorParser output. Unlike RazorParser, however, RazorCodeGenerator is an abstract base class from which language-specific implementations (such as CSharpRazorCodeGenerator and VBRazorCodeGenerator) derive. Razor API consumers reference the language-specific implementations that derive from RazorCodeGenerator, not RazorCodeGenerator directly.

System.Web.Razor.RazorEngineHost
> Contains the metadata required for creating Razor Templating Engines: things like the base class name and output class name (and namespace), as well as the assemblies and namespaces required to execute the generated template.

System.Web.Razor.RazorTemplateEngine
> Using configuration data provided by a RazorEngineHost, the Template Engine accepts a stream of text and transforms this text into .NET code (represented by a CodeCompileUnit) that gets compiled into a .NET type.

Custom Template Base Class
> Though not technically part of the Razor API, the Razor Templating Engine requires a custom template base class to use as a base class for the generated template

type. Without this class, the code that the Razor API generates will not compile and is effectively useless.

`System.CodeDom.Compiler.CodeDomProvider`

Also not technically part of the Razor API, the `CodeDomProvider` class compiles `CodeCompileUnits` into .NET types, making them available for .NET applications to consume. The Razor Templating API offers two `CodeDomProvider` implementations to compile `RazorTemplateEngine`-generated `CodeCompileUnits`: the `CSharpCodeProvider` and `VBCodeProvider`. As their names indicate, these two implementations compile C#-based and Visual Basic–based Razor templates respectively.

Configuring the Razor Template Engine

The `RazorTemplateEngine` class does most of the heavy lifting to transform Razor template text into usable .NET source code. Before creating an instance of the `RazorTemplateEngine`, however, the application must provide a set of properties that inform the engine about how to properly translate the Razor template text it receives. These properties come in the form of a `RazorEngineHost`.

Creating a RazorEngineHost

The code snippet below contains an example `RazorEngineHost` initialization:

```
var language = new CSharpRazorCodeLanguage();
var host = new RazorEngineHost(language) {
    DefaultBaseClass = "CustomTemplateBase",
    DefaultClassName = "DemoTemplate",
    DefaultNamespace = "ProgrammingRazor",
};
```

To begin, the `RazorEngineHost`'s constructor accepts a `RazorCodeLanguage` specifying the target template's code language. This example produces a host that can parse Razor templates written using C#. To support templates written in Visual Basic, supply a `VBRazorCodeLanguage` instance instead. The additional initializer properties instruct the code generator to emit code with a particular class name, deriving from a custom template base class, and residing in a particular namespace. Finally, add the `System` namespace to the list of imported namespaces required for the generated class to compile just as you would import a namespace in a normal, handwritten class.

The custom template base class—called `CustomTemplateBase` in this example—is somewhat special. Though it does not need to implement any "official" interface, the base class does need to provide methods with the following signatures:

public abstract void Execute()

Once populated with generated code, this method contains a series of calls to the Write methods to render the template contents.

void Write(object value) and void WriteLiteral(object value)

The `RazorTemplateEngine` populates the `Execute()` method with calls to the `Write()` and `WriteLiteral()` methods, much like using an `HtmlTextWriter` to render a Web Forms server control. While the `Execute()` method controls the flow of the template rendering, these two methods do the heavy lifting by converting objects and literal strings to rendered output.

This next code snippet contains the simplest possible implementation of a Razor template base class:

```
public abstract class CustomTemplateBase
{
  public abstract void Execute();

  public virtual void Write(object value)
  { /* Write value */ }

  public virtual void WriteLiteral(object value)
  { /* Write literal value */ }
}
```

While this implementation will, of course, do nothing to render any content, it is the minimum code required to successfully compile and execute a template class. By the end of this chapter we will revisit and expand upon this class, making it much more useful.

Creating the RazorTemplateEngine

Using the configuration provided in the previously created `RazorEngineHost`, this next example shows how straightforward it is to instantiate and generate code with a `Razor TemplateEngine`:

```
// Create a new Razor Template Engine
RazorTemplateEngine engine = new RazorTemplateEngine(host);

// Generate code for the template
GeneratorResults razorResult = engine.GenerateCode([TextReader]);
```

The `RazorTemplateEngine.GenerateCode()` method accepts `TextReader` parameters to provide the Razor template text and produces generated code in the form of `Generator Results`. This result class holds (among other things) a `CodeCompileUnit` representing the template's generated source code.

Compiling Razor Templates

The final step in the process of converting Razor text into an executable .NET class is compiling the generated source code into a .NET assembly, as shown below:

```
CompilerResults compilerResults =
  new CSharpCodeProvider()
    .CompileAssemblyFromDom(
```

```
        new CompilerParameters(/*...*/),
        razorResult.GeneratedCode
    );
```

The `CodeDomProvider.CompileAssemblyFromDom()` method converts the `CodeCompileUnit` from the previous steps (`razorResult.GeneratedCode`) and outputs the compiled types in the form of `CompilerResults`. The `CompilerResults` object contains plenty of interesting data describing the compiled output, including a reference to the assembly with the newly created template class type (in this example, the template class type is named `CustomTemplateBase`).

Executing a Razor Template

Configuring and compiling a Razor template produces a usable .NET type deriving from the base type specified in the `RazorEngineHost` properties. To process this template and render template output, simply create a new instance of the template type and execute it. Though there are several ways to create a new instance of a type, the `Activator.CreateInstance(Type)` function is the easiest (if perhaps not the most efficient) way.

Once you've created an instance of your custom Razor template type, simply call the `Execute()` method to execute the generated code:

```
var template = (CustomTemplateBase)Activator.CreateInstance(/*...*/);
template.Execute();
```

Congratulations, you have now leveraged the Razor API directly to manually create, compile, and execute your first Razor template class!

Advanced Templating Logic

Previously we discovered that, at a minimum, a valid Razor template base class must implement the `Execute()`, `Write()`, and `WriteLiteral()` methods. However, these methods are merely a starting point. Like any other .NET base class, template base classes can expose additional properties or methods to the template classes derived from them. This is how template base classes provide data and functionality to templates that derive from them.

For example, remember how the template shown in the beginning of the chapter referenced the `Posts` variable?

```
<div>
    @foreach(var post in Posts) {
        <div>@post.Title</div>
    }
</div>
```

For this template to compile and execute properly, the custom base class specified as the `RazorEngineHost.DefaultBaseClass` must expose a protected (or greater) access level

Posts property. Thus, to qualify as a base class for this template, a Posts property must be added to the CustomTemplateBase class. The result of this change can be seen in this snippet:

```
public abstract class CustomTemplateBase
{
    public IEnumerable<Post> Posts { get; set; }

    public abstract void Execute();

    protected void Write(object output) { /* Not shown */ }
    protected void WriteLiteral(object output) { /* Not shown */ }
}
```

As this next snippet demonstrates, the application can now assign a collection of Post objects to the template's Posts property prior to executing the template. With the Posts property set, the template produces the rendered text originally featured:

```
var template = (CustomTemplateBase)Activator.CreateInstance(/*...*/);
template.Posts = new BlogContext().Posts;
template.Execute();
```

CHAPTER 6

Advanced Techniques

Chapter 2 introduced you to two ways to create reusable markup: "Partial Views" on page 37 and "Razor Helpers" on page 41. Then Chapter 5 introduced you to the components that make up the Razor API and how they work together to help turn Razor templates into classes that render HTML to website visitors.

For most projects, partial views and Razor Helpers are all you need; however, some circumstances require a bit more customization. This chapter shows how to take the Razor API to the next level with several techniques that can help make application development with Razor templates quite a bit easier.

Inline Templates and Templated Delegates

Razor Helpers are an effective way to expose reusable code and markup as methods that the views in your application can share. Even though the Razor Helper syntax is pretty straightforward, Templated Delegates offer an even easier approach for accomplishing the same result, just with a different syntax.

As a reminder, here is an example snippet of a Razor Helper that renders an `<li>` list item:

```
@helper ListItem(string content) {
    <li>@content</li>
}

<ul>
    @foreach(var post in Posts) {
        @ListItem(post.Title)
    }
</ul>
```

And this is the same snippet as a Templated Delegate:

```
@{
    Func<dynamic, HelperResult> ListItem = @<li>@item</li>;
}
```

```
<ul>
    @foreach(var post in Posts) {
        @ListItem(post.Title)
    }
</ul>
```

The Templated Delegate is defined in a code block as a `Func<dynamic, HelperResult>` delegate, which is then called later in the markup. At first glance, there is very little difference between the Razor Helper and the Templated Delegate approaches. In fact, the code that uses them is exactly the same! The fact is, for scenarios like repeating a `<li>` tag, the differences really are arbitrary and deciding which approach to take is essentially a toss-up.

Where Templated Delegates really start to shine, however, is dealing with things like arrays and enumerations (i.e., iterations that use `foreach` loops). In these cases, you can eliminate most or all of the "boilerplate" code by incorporating it into the code of the Templated Delegate itself.

For instance, this is what the previous example would look like after incorporating the `foreach` iteration code into the Templated Delegate:

```
public static class RazorExtensions {
    public static HelperResult ApplyTemplate<T>(
            this IEnumerable<T> items, Func<T, HelperResult> template
    )
    {
        return new HelperResult(writer => {
            foreach (var item in items) {
                template(item).WriteTo(writer);
            }
        });
    }
}

<ul>
    @Posts.ApplyTemplate(
        @<li>@item</li>
    )
</ul>
```

The `RazorExtensions` class shown above combines the power of extension methods on top of generic `IEnumerable<T>` collections to efficiently apply a Templated Delegate to multiple items at the same time. The `foreach` loop is moved into the extension method and out of the web page markup. What's even more interesting is that the `<li>` tag markup is now passed into the `ApplyTemplate()` method as a parameter. The template markup is no different from the previous example, in which it was assigned to a variable, except in this case, instead of providing a reusable template, it offers a quick and easy way to pass a Razor snippet into a method.

The end result is that the web page view markup becomes much less imperative and much more declarative; for example, in this case, instead of saying "for each post, emit an `<li>` tag," the code says, "apply the `<li>` markup template to every post in the array."

Though the difference is subtle, the impact is significant: the view code is simplified and centralized. This makes the code easier to maintain over time, effectively applying updates to markup or logic across the entire site with a change to one place.

Sharing Views Between Projects

ASP.NET MVC makes it very easy to share views within the same website. Multiple controller actions can reference the same view when the shared view lives in the same folder as the other views for that controller or in the website's Shared folder. But how do you share views across projects?

Out of the box, there is no way to create a view in one project and reuse it in other projects. However, as you discovered in Chapter 5, Razor views are really just fancy designers that eventually generate .NET code, which can be compiled into assemblies, and compiled assemblies are certainly reusable across projects! Thus, what you need is a tool that can take the Razor views that you author in a separate project and run the Razor API directly against them to generate .NET code. Though this book gives you all the information you need to build a tool, the good news is that you don't have to: some folks in the open source community have already created it for you!

The Razor Single File Generator

The Razor Single File Generator (*http://razorgenerator.codeplex.com/*) is an open source Visual Studio extension that allows you to create reusable Razor views that aren't tied to any specific website. The extension lets you use Razor templates to generate classes much like the Visual Studio Settings designer and Windows Forms designer generate settings classes and Windows Forms classes.

Installing the Razor Single File Generator

Though the complete source code is hosted on CodePlex, the Razor Single File Generator installer is available in the Visual Studio Extensions Gallery, so the easiest way to get started with the Generator is to install it from the Gallery. To install, open the Visual Studio Extension Manager (Tools→Extension Manager…) and search the Online Gallery for "Razor Generator," as shown in Figure 6-1.

After the Razor Generator is installed (be sure to restart Visual Studio), create a new project to house the shared views. Outside of the fact that you will be applying a custom tool to your view files, there is nothing special about this new project; just create a new Class Library project (as shown in Figure 6-2) in the Blog solution that you've been working in and name it "ReusableComponents."

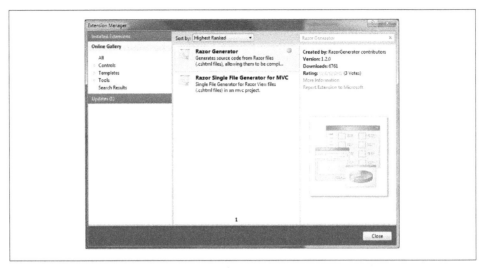

Figure 6-1. Installing the Razor Generator in the Extension Manager

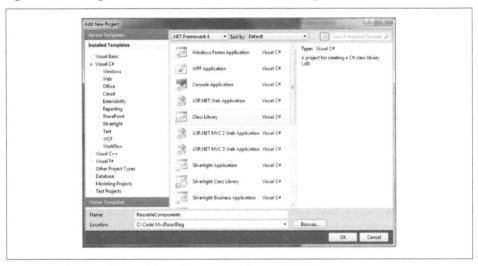

Figure 6-2. Creating the new Class Library project for reusable views

Creating Reusable ASP.NET MVC Views

One of the most common scenarios for a view that is shared across projects is a generic error page, so let's create one and see how the Razor Single File Generator handles ASP.NET MVC views.

Creating reusable ASP.NET MVC views with the Razor Single File Generator is almost the same as creating views within an ASP.NET MVC project itself. When you create a folder structure similar to the ~/Views folder convention that ASP.NET MVC expects, the only thing you have to do is associate the views with the Razor Single File Generator by setting each view's Custom Tool property to `RazorGenerator`.

Since the new ReusableComponents class library is not an ASP.NET MVC project, it will not have the ~/*Views* folder, so go ahead and create one. The new view you are about to add will be used across multiple controllers, so the class library's folder structure should reflect this: create another directly under ~/*Views* named "Shared," mirroring the ASP.NET MVC application folder convention. When you're done, the ReusableComponents class library should look like Figure 6-3.

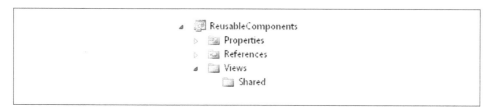

Figure 6-3. Reusable Components project with the ~/Views folder structure

Now that the folder structure is in place, add a new file named *GenericError.cshtml* to the Shared folder using the Add→New Item... content menu. Since the project is a Class Library project and not an ASP.NET MVC, Visual Studio will refuse to show the MVC 3 View Page (Razor) item type. That's OK; just choose another plain-content item type, such as Text File or HTML Page. Since your new item (*GenericError.cshtml*) has the .cshtml file extension, Visual Studio will know that it is a Razor template.

Though Visual Studio recognizes the new file as a Razor template, you need to tell the Razor Single File Generator to start generating code from that template. To wire up the Generator, open up the properties for the *GenericError.cshtml* file and set its Custom Tool property to `RazorGenerator`. Figure 6-4 shows a properly configured Razor Generator.

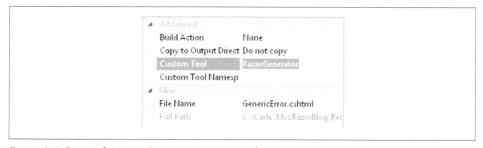

Figure 6-4. Setting the RazorGenerator Custom Tool property

Completely replace all content (if any) in the new *GenericError.cshtml* file with the following Razor markup:

```
@{ Layout = null; }
<html>
<head>
    <title>Website Error!</title>
    <style>
        body { text-align: center; background-color: #6CC5C3; }
        .error-details .stack-trace { display: none; }
        .error-details:hover .stack-trace { display: block; }
    </style>
</head>
<body>
    <h2>We're sorry, but our site has encountered an error!</h2>
    <img src="http://bit.ly/pjnXyE" />

@if (ViewData["ErrorMessage"] != null) {
    <div class="error-details">
        <h2>@ViewData["ErrorMessage"]</h2>
        <div class="stack-trace">@ViewData["StackTrace"]</div>
    </div>
}
</body>
</html>
```

Immediately after you specify the Custom Tool property, you should see that the Razor Single File Generator has generated the class *GenericError.cs*, grouped underneath *GenericError.cshtml* (as shown in Figure 6-5).

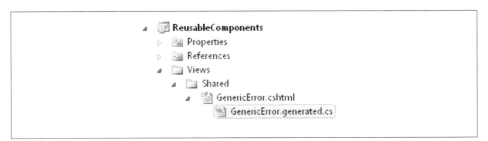

Figure 6-5. New file generated by the Razor Generator

 If you do not see the generated file, something has gone wrong! Be sure that you have spelled the name of the custom tool correctly (RazorGen erator with no spaces). If it still does not work, try going back and following the steps from the beginning of this section. Make sure that you restart Visual Studio after installing the Razor Generator tool and check all the installation logs to make sure that there were no errors during installation.

Feel free to open this new file and inspect its generated contents. It should look pretty similar to code that the Razor API generated in Chapter 5, modified to work with the ASP.NET MVC framework. The generated code acts like any other code, compiling into an assembly that you can share with any number of websites.

Including precompiled views in an ASP.NET MVC web application

After following the steps in this section, you are left with a project library filled with precompiled ASP.NET MVC Razor views...now what? Because of the standard conventions the ASP.NET MVC Razor View Engine uses, the view engine will not be able to locate views outside of its standard search paths (the Views folders in the ASP.NET MVC web application), so it has no idea that your precompiled views even exist, let alone how to execute them.

The answer to this situation is the `PrecompiledMvcEngine`, a custom view engine built by the Razor Single File Generator developers that extends the core Razor View Engine to look for precompiled views. The easiest way to begin using the `PrecompiledMvcEngine` is to use the NuGet Package Manager (see "Using the NuGet Package Manager" on page 57) to install the PrecompiledMvcEngine package to the class library project that contains your precompiled views. The PrecompiledMvcEngine package adds several artifacts to your project:

Several web.config files
> The Razor API and Visual Studio Razor IntelliSense assume that Razor views live within a web application project, and they read their configuration information from the project's *web.config* files. Even though your project is a class library project, the *web.config* files that the PrecompiledMvcEngine package adds give Visual Studio enough information to enable Razor IntelliSense, even for views that use the Razor Single File Generator.

A sample Razor view
> The PrecompiledMvcEngine package adds a sample Razor view named *Test.cshtml* in the project's *~/Views/Home* folder to show how precompiled views should be configured. If everything is working properly, you should see this view generate a code-behind (*Test.cs*) file immediately. The *Test.cshtml* view is just a reference, so you can modify it as you wish, rename it, or even delete it entirely.

~/App_Start/PrecompiledMvcViewEngineStart.cs
> Though its name is not important, the *PrecompiledMvcViewEngineStart.cs* file contains logic (shown below) that tells your ASP.NET MVC application to use the `PrecompiledMvcEngine` for all the precompiled Razor views in this class library project. The *PrecompiledMvcViewEngineStart.cs* file also includes the `WebActivator.PreApplicationStartMethod` attribute, which tells the WebActivator library to execute the `PrecompiledMvcViewEngineStart.Start()` method when the web application starts up, registering the `PrecompiledMvcEngine` in the web application's `ViewEngines` collection:

```
[assembly: WebActivator.PreApplicationStartMethod(
    typeof(ReusableComponents.App_Start.PrecompiledMvcViewEngineStart),
    "Start"
)]

public static class PrecompiledMvcViewEngineStart {
    public static void Start() {
```

```
var currentAssembly = typeof(PrecompiledMvcViewEngineStart).Assembly;
var engine = new PrecompiledMvcEngine(currentAssembly);
ViewEngines.Engines.Insert(0, engine);
VirtualPathFactoryManager.RegisterVirtualPathFactory(engine);
        }
    }
```

Once the PrecompiledMvcViewEngine NuGet package is installed and you've moved the ~/*Views/Home/Index.cshtml* file from the sample blog site to the ReusableComponents class library project, you should be able to run the website and see that everything works just as it did before. ASP.NET MVC now executes the precompiled *Index.cshtml* file from the class library, not caring that the file did not exist in its local ~/ *Views* folder. But how did the PrecompiledMvcViewEngine know which view to render?

We've seen that the PrecompiledMvcViewEngine knows how to render precompiled Razor views in an ASP.NET MVC application and the PrecompiledMvcViewEngineStart takes care of registering the PrecompiledMvcViewEngine with the web application, so there is only one missing piece in the puzzle: locating the precompiled view. Though it may be surprising, PrecompiledMvcViewEngine still relies on the ASP.NET MVC Views folder convention, using relative file paths to locate the views. However, this is slightly misleading. The PrecompiledMvcViewEngine doesn't look at physical files; it looks for the System.Web.WebPages.PageVirtualPathAttribute that the Razor Single File Generator adds to every view that it generates that includes the view's relative file path.

The following shows the first few lines of the sample view *Test.cshtml* that includes that PageVirtualPathAttribute:

```
[System.Web.WebPages.PageVirtualPathAttribute("~/Views/Home/Test.cshtml")]
public class Test : System.Web.Mvc.WebViewPage<dynamic>
```

Since the virtual path name is relative, whether the ~/*Views/Home/Test.cshtml* view resides in the ASP.NET MVC application or the class library project, its virtual path is the same. Thus, when the ASP.NET MVC application requests the Test view in the Home controller, the PrecompiledMvcViewEngine knows to use the precompiled *Test.cshtml* view registered with the virtual path ~/*Views/Home/Test.cshtml*.

Be sure to add the PrecompiledMvcEngine package to the class library project that contains your precompiled views, *not* your ASP.NET MVC web application project. Your web application will need the PrecompiledMvcEngine assembly at runtime, but the artifacts that the NuGet package installs to your package are only meant for class library projects that contained precompiled Razor views.

Creating Reusable ASP.NET MVC Helpers

You can also apply the Razor Single File Generator to Razor templates that include Razor Helpers to produce a result similar to as if the templates resided in an ASP.NET MVC application's App_Code folder.

The Razor Single File Generator expects Razor Helper templates to live in the ~/Views/ Helpers folder, so before you can create any helpers, you'll need to create this folder. After you create the Helpers folder, follow the same steps you followed earlier to add a Razor template file to the new Helpers folder. Name the file *TwitterHelpers.cshtml*. Then set the Custom Tool property to RazorGenerator, just as you did for the ASP.NET MVC view template.

Immediately after setting the property, you should see the autogenerated file *Twitter-Helpers.cs*. Open the file and take a look: the Razor Generator has successfully parsed the empty Razor template and generated a C# class for us, ready to hold some Helper functions. An empty class doesn't do us any good, however, so let's create a helper function using the standard Razor syntax that we used to create the TweetButton Helper Method (see "Razor Helpers" on page 41). As a matter of fact, just go ahead and copy the contents of that file:

```
@helper TweetButton(string url, string text) {
    <script src="http://platform.twitter.com/widgets.js" type="text/javascript">
    </script>
    <div>
        <a href="http://twitter.com/share" class="twitter-share-button"
            data-url="@url" data-text="'@text'">Tweet</a>
    </div>
}
```

Saving the file and switching back to the generated *TwitterHelpers.cs* file shows that's it's been updated again in real time. This time the static helper class contains the code for our custom TweetButton Helper. Example 6-1 contains the complete autogenerated code.[*]

Example 6-1. Auto-Generated MvcHelper Code

```
namespace ReusableComponents.Views.Helpers
{
    using System;
    using System.Collections.Generic;
    using System.IO;
    using System.Linq;
    using System.Net;
    using System.Text;
    using System.Web;
    using System.Web.Helpers;
    using System.Web.Mvc;
    using System.Web.Mvc.Ajax;
    using System.Web.Mvc.Html;
    using System.Web.Routing;
    using System.Web.Security;
    using System.Web.UI;
    using System.Web.WebPages;

    [System.CodeDom.Compiler.GeneratedCodeAttribute("RazorGenerator", "1.1.0.0")]
```

---

[*] The comments and some whitespace have been removed for better readability

```
    public static class TwitterHelpers
    {
        public static System.Web.WebPages.HelperResult
                            TweetButton(string url, string text) {
            return new System.Web.WebPages.HelperResult(__razor_helper_writer => {
                WebViewPage.WriteLiteralTo(@__razor_helper_writer,
                    "<script src=\"http://platform.twitter.com/widgets.js\" "+
                    "type=\"text/javascript\">" +
                    "</script>\r\n");

                WebViewPage.WriteLiteralTo(@__razor_helper_writer,
                    "<div>\r\n" +
                    "<a href=\"http://twitter.com/share\" "+
                    "class=\"twitter-share-button data-url=\""
                );

                WebViewPage.WriteTo(@__razor_helper_writer, url);

                WebViewPage.WriteLiteralTo(@__razor_helper_writer, "\" data-text=\"\'");

                WebViewPage.WriteTo(@__razor_helper_writer, text);

                WebViewPage.WriteLiteralTo(@__razor_helper_writer,
                    "\'\">Tweet</a>\r\n" +
                    "</div>\r\n"
                );
            });
        }
    }
}
```

With the autogenerated class in place, ASP.NET MVC websites that reference the Re-usableComponents assembly will be able to use the TweetButton Helper just like any other Helper method defined in the website's App_Code folder. For example:

```
@using ReusableComponents.Views.Helpers
<div>
    @TwitterHelpers.TweetButton(url, message)
</div>
```

Razor Single File Generator Generator Implementations

The Razor Generator tool is actually a shell that hosts several different kinds of generators. All of them leverage the core Razor API, much like you saw in Chapter 5, though each generator uses a different implementation to generate code that targets specific scenarios.

As of this writing, the Razor Generator includes the following generators:

MvcHelper
    Creates a static type that is best suited for writing MVC-specific helper methods.

`MvcView`

Creates a WebViewPage which allows the use of precompiled MVC views.

`WebPage`

Creates a WebPage type that can be used as a WebPages Application Part (such as Admin and RazorDebugger).

`WebPagesHelper`

Creates a HelperPage type that is suited for precompiling and distributing Web-Pages helper.

`Template`

Generator based on T4 preprocessed template.

You've seen the first two—`MvcHelper` and `MvcView`—in action already. The Razor Single File Generator figured out which generator to use based on the file's location in the site. By virtue of the fact that the *GenericError.cshtml* file is in the *~/Views/Shared* folder, the Generator assumes that the file is an ASP.NET MVC view, so it uses the `MvcHelper` generator implementation to generate the code file. Likewise, the Generator assumes that files in the *~/Views/Helpers* folder are ASP.NET MVC Helpers and uses the `MvcHelper` generator implementation.

The Razor Single File Generator offers an alternative method (which looks like this: `@* Generator: MvcHelper *@`) to explicitly specify which generator implementation it should use to generate code for a given Razor template.

The following example shows how you can tell the Razor Single File Generator to generate code for a WebMatrix WebPages Application Part:

```
@* Generator: WebPage *@
<div>The time is: @DateTime.Now</div>
```

The generator declaration always takes precedence when it is specified, even when the Razor template file resides in a folder that falls under a different collection. Thus, you can store your Razor template however you like and let the Razor Single File Generator know which templates should be handled differently.

Unit Testing Razor Views

Many best practices advocate keeping the logic in your views as limited and simple as possible; however, the ability to execute unit tests against Razor-based MVC views can still be beneficial in some scenarios.

Take a look at the code snippet for an example of an ASP.NET MVC Razor view:

```
<p>
    Order ID:
    <span id='order-id'>@Model.OrderID</span>
</p>
<p>
    Customer:
```

```
@(Html.ActionLink(
        @Model.CustomerName,
        "Details", "Customer",
        new { id = @Model.CustomerID },
        null))
</p>
```

The default ASP.NET MVC Razor view class exposes properties such as `Model` and `Html` that this view relies on. Thus, in order to compile and execute the view outside of the ASP.NET MVC runtime, you must create a custom template base class that implements these properties as well. This next example contains a snippet from the `OrderIn foTemplateBase`, modified to include the `Model` and `Html` properties so that it may be used to compile the previous view:

```
public abstract class OrderInfoTemplateBase
{
    public CustomerOrder Model { get; set; }
    public HtmlHelper Html { get; set; }
        ...
}
```

The `OrderInfoTemplateBase` class now fulfills the template's dependencies on the ASP.NET MVC base classes, allowing the `OrderInfoTemplateBase` to act as a stand-in for the ASP.NET MVC base classes. Introducing custom base classes such as `OrderIn foTemplateBase` provides complete control over the properties and functionality provided to the template. Custom base classes also alleviate the need to execute ASP.NET MVC views within the ASP.NET MVC runtime.

Example 6-2 shows the power of swapping production components with mock objects.

Example 6-2. Unit test executing a Razor template instance using mock objects

```
public void ShouldRenderLinkToCustomerDetails()
{
    var mockHtmlHelper = new Moq.Mock<HtmlHelper>();
    var order = new CustomerOrder()
        {
            OrderID = 1234,
            CustomerName = "Homer Simpson",
        };

    // Create the instance and set the properties
    var template = (OrderInfoTemplateBase)Activator.CreateInstance(/*...*/);

    template.Html = mockHtmlHelper.Object;
    template.Model = customerOrder;

    template.Execute();

    // Verify that the link was generated
    mockHtmlHelper.Verify(htmlHelper =>
        htmlHelper.ActionLink(
            order.CustomerName,
            "Details", "Customer",
```

```
        It.IsAny<object>()
    );
}
```

By replacing the production `HtmlHelper` class with a mock implementation, the unit test can easily make assertions against—and therefore confirm the validity of—code in the view without relying on the ASP.NET MVC runtime.

 If you are using the Razor Single File Generator to create reusable views, you do not need to use reflection-based approaches such as `Activa tor.CreateInstance()`. Since the Razor Single File Generator generates actual classes, all you need to do is create a new instance of the class (e.g., `var template = new CustomerOrderTemplate();`) and run tests against the new instance.

The ability to inject mock and stub objects to take the place of production types is a great boon for unit tests. Without this ability, most sites must resort to running all UI tests through slow and unreliable browser-based testing. In stark contrast, injecting mock and stub objects allows developers to create unit tests that execute in mere milliseconds.

Applying Razor to Text-Based Scenarios

Chapter 5 walks you through the life cycle of a Razor template and how the Razor API converts template text into an executable class. The WebMatrix and ASP.NET MVC frameworks leverage the Razor syntax and the Razor API as a way for developers to define how HTML should be rendered for a web page. However, Chapter 5 shows that it's relatively straightforward to execute the Razor API outside of WebMatrix or ASP.NET MVC, allowing you to leverage the Razor syntax in your own applications. Not only is it straightforward, but Razor templates can output much more than just HTML, which makes Razor suitable for many templating tasks.

Though Chapter 5 explains everything you need to leverage the Razor API directly, let's run though an example to show it in action, using Razor templates to drive a theoretical custom email mail merging application. We'll start with a sample email template and build what we need to turn it into a .NET class that the mail merge application can execute to generate email text:

```
Hello, @ServiceRequest.CustomerName!

Thank you for requesting more information about
@ServiceRequest.ServiceName on @ServiceRequest.CreateDateDisplayValue.
Please find the information you requested below
and we look forward to hearing from you again!

@ServiceRequest.DetailedInformation
```

```
Sincerely,
@ServiceRequest.SenderInformation

[ Information current as of @DateTime.Now ]
```

Though the custom mail merge application is not an ASP.NET MVC application, creating a model to hold all the data that the template needs makes it much easier to pass data to the template when it is rendering. The following shows the model class that contains all of the properties that the template needs:

```
public class ServiceRequestEmailModel
{
    public string SenderEmail { get; set; }
    public string CustomerEmail { get; set; }

    public string CustomerName { get; set; }
    public DateTime CreateDate { get; set; }
    public string DetailedInformation { get; set; }
    public string SenderInformation { get; set; }
    public string ServiceName { get; set; }

    // Wrap the CreateDate value in a property that
    // provides a formatted display value to the view.
    // This way, the formatting logic can be centralized
    // and stay out of the view.
    public string CreateDateDisplayValue
    {
        get { return CreateDate.ToString("G"); }
    }
}
```

Next, the generated class will need a base class that implements the Write() and Write Literal() methods. The next example contains the full Razor email template base class necessary to compile the template text:

```
namespace RazorTemplateMailer
{
    using System.Net.Mail;
    using System.Text;

    public abstract class ServiceRequestEmailGeneratorBase
    {
        private StringBuilder _buffer;

        public string SenderEmail { get; set; }

        protected ServiceRequestEmailModel ServiceRequest { get; private set; }

        public MailMessage GenerateMailMessage(ServiceRequestEmailModel model)
        {
            // Update the model reference
            ServiceRequest = model;

            // Clear any existing buffered content
            _buffer = new StringBuilder();
```

```
            // Render the template to the buffer
            Execute();

            // Return a new Mail Message with the buffer contents
            return new MailMessage(SenderEmail, model.CustomerEmail)
                    {
                        Body = _buffer.ToString()
                    };
        }

        public abstract void Execute();

        public void Write(object value)
        {
            WriteLiteral(value);
        }

        public void WriteLiteral(object value)
        {
            _buffer.Append(value);
        }
    }
}
```

Notice how the ServiceRequestEmailGeneratorBase class's Write() methods populate a string buffer. After it's done populating the buffer, the class then converts the buffered text into the body of a new System.Net.Mail.MailMessage. This particular base class remains happily unaware of how its descendants call the Write() methods. In fact, it knows nothing about the Razor Templating API at all!

The following example shows the template in action in the form of an application that pulls customer service requests from a database and sends the customer a custom email generated from the Razor template:

Custom application using the Razor API

```
        public void EmailServiceRequests()
        {
            // Get Service Requests from the database
            var requests = ServiceRequests.GetAll();

            // Map the database data to the email model
            var serviceRequestEmailModels =
                from request in requests
                select new ServiceRequestEmailModel
                    {
                        CustomerName = request.CustomerName,
                        CreateDate = request.CreateDate,
                        DetailedInformation = request.Information,
                        SenderEmail = request.CustomerEmailAddress,
                        SenderInformation = request.SenderInformation,
                        ServiceName = request.ServiceName,
                    };
```

```
// Get an instance of the compiled template
Type generatorType = Type.GetType("RazorDemo.ServiceRequestEmailGenerator");
var emailGenerator =

(ServiceRequestEmailGeneratorBase)Activator.CreateInstance(emailGeneratorType);

// Supply any required properties
emailGenerator.SenderEmail = "mailmerger@bigcorp.com";

// Execute the template for each model
// and send the email to the customer
SmtpClient smtp = new SmtpClient();
foreach (var emailModel in serviceRequestEmailModels)
{
    var email = emailGenerator.GenerateMailMessage(emailModel);
    smtp.Send(email);
}
}
```

This application retrieves template data from a database and executes an instance of the ServiceRequestEmailGeneratorBase template class against each set of data, producing the previously discussed email message as a result. The application then sends the resulting email to the user via the System.Net.Mail.SmtpClient:

```
Hello, Homer Simpson!

Thank you for requesting more information about
Donuts on 1/15/2011 11:04:12 AM.
Please find the information you requested below
and we look forward to hearing from you again!

  Donuts are delicious!

Sincerely,
Big Corp.

[ Information current as of 1/15/2011 11:04 AM ]
```

It seems email generation applications like this get built time and time again, each implementation drastically different from the next. Since this approach leverages standardized and well-documented components of the .NET Framework, the resulting solution becomes easy for any developer to understand and maintain.

CHAPTER 7

Conclusion

At first glance, many consider Razor to be just another way to generate HTML. Hopefully, the examples in this book have shown that Razor is far more than a simple markup syntax. Razor is a versatile templating framework that can power simple websites or complex applications. What's more, Razor's extensible API lets developers further customize their environments, helping to make their applications easier to create and maintain.

The next time you sit down to evaluate which ASP.NET MVC View Engine or templating platform is the best fit for your next application, consider the benefits that Razor and its API offer. You may be pleasantly surprised!

About the Author

Jess Chadwick is an independent software consultant specializing in web technologies. He has over a decade of development experience ranging from embedded devices in startups to enterprise-scale web farms at Fortune 500 companies. He is an ASPInsider, a Microsoft MVP in ASP.NET, and an avid community member, frequently delivering technical presentations as well as leading the NJDOTNET Central New Jersey .NET user group. Jess lives in the Philadelphia area with his wonderful wife, baby daughter, and black Lab.

Get even more for your money.

Join the O'Reilly Community, and register the O'Reilly books you own. It's free, and you'll get:

- $4.99 ebook upgrade offer
- 40% upgrade offer on O'Reilly print books
- Membership discounts on books and events
- Free lifetime updates to ebooks and videos
- Multiple ebook formats, DRM FREE
- Participation in the O'Reilly community
- Newsletters
- Account management
- 100% Satisfaction Guarantee

Signing up is easy:

1. **Go to: oreilly.com/go/register**
2. **Create an O'Reilly login.**
3. **Provide your address.**
4. **Register your books.**

Note: English-language books only

To order books online:
oreilly.com/store

For questions about products or an order:
orders@oreilly.com

To sign up to get topic-specific email announcements and/or news about upcoming books, conferences, special offers, and new technologies:
elists@oreilly.com

For technical questions about book content:
booktech@oreilly.com

To submit new book proposals to our editors:
proposals@oreilly.com

O'Reilly books are available in multiple DRM-free ebook formats. For more information:
oreilly.com/ebooks

O'REILLY®

Spreading the knowledge of innovators | oreilly.com

The information you need, when and where you need it.

With Safari Books Online, you can:

Access the contents of thousands of technology and business books

- Quickly search over 7000 books and certification guides
- Download whole books or chapters in PDF format, at no extra cost, to print or read on the go
- Copy and paste code
- Save up to 35% on O'Reilly print books
- **New!** Access mobile-friendly books directly from cell phones and mobile devices

Stay up-to-date on emerging topics before the books are published

- Get on-demand access to evolving manuscripts.
- Interact directly with authors of upcoming books

Explore thousands of hours of video on technology and design topics

- Learn from expert video tutorials
- Watch and replay recorded conference sessions

Spreading the knowledge of innovators   safari.oreilly.com

Lightning Source UK Ltd.
Milton Keynes UK
UKHW032002050219
336801UK00005B/299/P